Praying That Receives Answers

E.M. BOUNDS

WHITAKER
HOUSE

Unless otherwise indicated, all Scripture quotations are taken from the *King James Version* (KJV) of the Holy Bible.

PRAYING THAT RECEIVES ANSWERS
formerly titled: *Obtaining Answers to Prayer*

ISBN: 0-88368-594-9
Printed in the United States of America
Copyright © 1984 by Whitaker House

Whitaker House
30 Hunt Valley Circle
New Kensington, PA 15068

CONTENTS

INTRODUCTION

Rev. Edward McKendrie Bounds was passionately devoted to his beloved Lord and Savior, Jesus Christ. His devotion was extraordinary in that he was always praying and writing about Him, except when he was sleeping.

God gave Bounds a large heart and an insatiable desire to serve Him. To this end he enjoyed inspiration. Otherwise, he could never have brought things out of his treasury which far exceed most modern Christian writing.

Bounds is easily the brightest star of the devotional sky. There is no man who, since the days of the apostles, has surpassed the depth of his marvelous research into the life of prayer.

He was busily writing his manuscripts when the Lord said to him, "Well done, thou good and faithful servant, enter thou into the joys of thy Lord." He often wrote to me saying, "Pray for me that God will give me new nerves and new visions to finish the manuscripts."

Bounds was meek and humble, and never did we know him to retaliate on any of his enemies. He cried over them and wept, praying for them unceasingly.

No man could fool Bounds. He was a diagnostician of rare ability. Bounds shied away from all frauds in profession and would waste no time upon them.

Though comparatively unknown for many years, E.M. Bounds is now becoming the mighty Amazon of the devotional world.

John Wesley once said, "The world is my parish," but E.M. Bounds prayed as if the universe was his zone.

Bounds was the incarnation of unearthliness, humility, and self-denial, and he will live in the hearts of saints for everlasting ages.

Homer W. Hodge

Chapter 1

FAITH IN PRAYER

"The Holy Spirit will give the praying saint the brightness of an immortal hope, the music of a deathless song. In His baptism and communion with the heart, He will give sweeter and more enlarged visions of heaven until the taste for other things will fade, and other visions will grow dim and distant. He will put notes of other worlds in human hearts until all earth's music is discord and songless"—Rev. E.M. Bounds.

The men and women of the Old Testament saw God as their Father and felt that prayerful communion with Him was a natural part of life. Israel's leaders were noted for their habit of coming to their Father in prayer. Prayer and God's loving and powerful answer to it is a major theme of the Old Testament.

The tenth chapter of Joshua describes God's powerful intervention in a prolonged battle between the Israelites and their enemies as a result of prayer. Night was rapidly coming on, and the Israelites discovered that they needed a few more hours of daylight to ensure victory. Joshua, that sturdy man of God, stepped into the breach with prayer for the Lord's army.

The sun was setting too rapidly for God's people to reap the full fruits of a great victory. Joshua, seeing how much depended on the occasion, cried out in the sight and hearing of Israel, "Sun, stand thou still upon Gideon; and thou, Moon, in the valley of Ajalon" (Joshua 10:12). The sun actually stood still, and the moon stopped in its course at the command of this praying man of God, until the Lord's people had avenged themselves upon His enemies.

God's Provision For Jacob

Jacob's life was not a strict pattern of righteousness, prior to his all-night praying. Yet, he was a man of prayer and trusted in the God of prayer. He was swift to call upon God in prayer when he was in trouble because he knew God would answer him. For example, as Jacob fled from Esau, he prayed. As night came on, he found a special place where he could sleep peacefully. That night he had a wonderful dream in which he saw the angels of God ascending and descending on a ladder which stretched from earth to heaven. It was no wonder that he awoke exclaiming, "Surely the Lord is in this place and I knew it not" (Genesis 28:16).

As a result of this dream, he entered into a very definite covenant with Almighty God. In prayer Jacob vowed to the Lord, saying, "If God will be with me, and will keep me in this way that I go, and will give me bread to eat and raiment to put on, so that I come again to my father's house in peace; and shall the Lord be my God, and this stone which I have set for a pillar shall be God's house; and of all that Thou shalt give me, I will surely give one-tenth unto Thee" (Genesis 28:20-22).

With a deep sense of his utter dependence on God, Jacob conditioned his prayer for protection, blessing, and guidance with a solemn vow. Thus Jacob supported his prayer to God with a vow.

Twenty years passed while Jacob stayed at Laban's house. He married two of Laban's daughters, and God gave him children. God had generously answered Jacob's prayer. Becoming very wealthy, Jacob decided to leave Laban's house and return home. Nearing home it occurred to him that he must meet his brother Esau, whose anger had not abated despite the passage of time. God, however, had said to him, "Return to thy father's house and to thy kindred, and I will be with thee" (Genesis 31:3).

In this dire emergency, no doubt God's promise and the vow he had made long ago came to mind. As a result, he prayed all night. We notice that this is the night of that strange, inexplicable incident of the angel struggling with Jacob all night long, until Jacob at last obtained the victory. "I will not let thee go except thou bless me" (Genesis 32:26). Immediately in answer to his fervent prayer, God responded by blessing Jacob richly and changing his name. God, knowing the desire of Jacob's heart, blessed Jacob further by removing Esau's angry nature. When Jacob and Esau met the next day, Esau greeted the brother who had wronged him with kindness and generosity. The remarkable change in the heart of Esau could only have come through prayer.

Hannah's Prayer

Samuel, a mighty intercessor for Israel and a man of God, was the product of his mother's prayer. Hannah is a memorable example of the nature and benefits of persistent praying. She had no children, and she especially yearned for a son. Her whole soul was in her desire. So she went to the house of worship and saw Eli, God's priest.

Staggering under the weight of her longing, she could not articulate her desires. Nonetheless, she poured out her soul in prayer before the Lord (see 1 Samuel 1:10-17). Her silent prayer was so fervent that Eli thought she was drunk. When Eli learned the truth about Hannah's prayer, he said, ''and the God of Israel grant thee thy petition.'' Soon Samuel was hers by a conscious faith, and a nation was restored by faith.

Samuel was born in answer to the faithful Hannah's prayer. The solemn covenant which she made with God if He would grant her request must not be left out of this investigation of a praying woman and the answer she received. Prayer in its highest form of faith is prayer which carries the whole man as a sacrificial offering. Thus, devoting the whole man to God—with a quenchless and impassioned desire for heaven—mightily helps praying.

Nothing Is Beyond God's Reach

Samson is somewhat of a paradox when we examine his religious character. Despite all of his extreme faults, he knew the God who hears prayer, and he knew how to talk to God.

Israel could never slip so far away, fall into sin so deeply, or be bound so strongly that God could not easily span the distance, fathom the depths, and break the chains at their cry. The lesson they were always learning and always forgetting was that prayer continually brought God to their deliverance and that there was nothing too hard for God to do for His people.

We find all of God's saints in distress at different times in some way or another. Their troubles are, however, often the heralds of their great triumphs. But no matter what the reason, the kind, the degree, or the source, no difficult circumstances could keep God from answering prayer. Not even the great strength of Samson could relieve him of his distress. The Scriptures say:

"And when he came unto Lehi, the Philistines shouted against him: and the Spirit of the Lord came mightily upon him, and the cords that were upon his arms became as flax that was burnt with fire, and his bands loosed from off his hands.

"And he found a new jawbone of an ass, and put forth his hand, and took it, and slew a thousand men therewith.

"And Samson said, With the jawbone of an ass, heaps upon heaps, with the jawbone of an ass have I slain a thousand men.

"And it came to pass, when he had made an end of speaking, that he cast away the jawbone out of his hand, and called that place Ramath-lehi.

"And he was sore a thirst, and called on the Lord, and said, Thou hast given this great deliverance into the hand of Thy servant: and now shall I die of thirst, and fall into the hand of the uncircumcised?

"But God clave a hollow place that was in the jaw, and there came water thereout; and when he had drunk, his spirit came again, and he revived" (Judges 15:14-19).

Another incident in Samson's life shows how, during a great trial, a saint's mind involuntarily turns to God in prayer. However checkered their spiritual life, however far from God they depart, however sinful they might be, when trouble came upon these men they invariably called upon God for deliverance, knowing He would answer them. As a rule when they repent God hears their cries and grants their requests.

The incident in question comes at the close of Samson's life. Read the record in the sixteenth chapter of Judges. Samson had formed an alliance with Delilah, a heathen woman. In connivance with the Philistines, she sought to discover the source of his immense strength. Three successive times she failed.

At last, by her persistence, she persuaded Samson to divulge the wonderful secret. In an unsuspecting hour he told her that the source of his strength was in his hair which had never been cut. That night she robbed him of his great physical power by cutting off his hair. She then called for the Philistines who came, tortured him, and put out his eyes.

Later when the Philistines were gathered together to offer a great sacrifice to Dagon, their idol god, they called for Samson to entertain them. The following is the account as he stood there presumably the laughing-stock of his enemies and God's enemies.

"And Samson said unto the lad that held him by the hand, Suffer me that I may feel the pillars whereupon the house standeth, that I may lean upon them.

"Now the house was full of men and women; and all the lords of the Philistines were there; and there were upon the roof about three thousand men and women, that beheld while Samson made sport.

"And Samson called unto the Lord, and said, O Lord God, remember me, I pray Thee, and strengthen me, I pray Thee, only this once, O God, that I may be at once avenged of the Philistines for my two eyes. And Samson took hold of the two middle pillars upon which the house stood, and on which it was borne up, of the one with his right hand, and of the other with his left.

"And Samson said, Let me die with the Philistines. And he bowed himself with all his might; and the house fell upon the lords, and upon all the people that were therein. So the dead which he slew at his death were more than they which he slew in his life'' (Judges 16:26-30).

God's praying saints of the Old Testament found their comfort and their strength in their believing petitions to the Father. Prayer and God's answers compose a vital part of the Old Testament.

Chapter 2

MIGHTY ANSWERS TO PRAYER

"Bishops Lambeth and Wainwright had a great mission meeting in Osaka, Japan. One day the order came from Japanese officials that Christian meetings were no longer allowed in the city. Lambeth and Wainwright did all they could, but the officials were unrelenting. The bishops then retired to the prayer room. Supper time arrived and the Japanese servant girl came to summon them to their meal, and she fell under the power of prayer. Mrs. Lambeth came to find out was happening, and she fell under the same power. They then rose, went to the mission hall, and immediately started a prayer meeting. God fell upon the assembly causing two sons of the city officials to come to the altar and be saved. The next morning one of the officials in authority came to the mission and said, 'Go on with your meetings, you will not be interrupted.' The Osaka daily paper came out with the headline 'The Christian's God Came To Town Last Night' "—Rev. H.C. Morrison.

Jonah, the man who prayed in the whale's belly brings to mind another remarkable instance of Old Testament saints who were convinced of the power of prayer. Jonah, a prophet of the Lord, was a fugitive from God running from his place of duty. He had been sent on a mission to warn the wicked city of Nineveh. He was commanded to cry out against them, "for their wickedness is come up before Me" said God (Jonah 1:2).

But Jonah, through fear or otherwise, decided not to obey God. He boarded a ship leaving for Tarshish—thinking he could flee from God. Jonah overlooked the fact that the same God who had sent him on that alarming mission had His eye upon him as he hid himself on board the vessel.

A storm arose as the vessel was on its way to Tarshish. The crew decided to throw Jonah overboard in order to appease God and to avert the destruction of the boat and everyone on board. God, however, was still there with Jonah as He had been from the beginning. God had prepared a whale to swallow Jonah in order to stop his flight from his post of duty and to save Jonah so he would carry out His will.

Mighty Prayer Brings Results

Jonah, while in the whale's belly, suffered a strange and terrifying experience and called upon God. God heard him and caused the whale to vomit Jonah out on dry land. What possible force could have rescued him from this fearful place?

He seemed hopelessly lost, in "the belly of hell" (see Jonah 2:2). But he prayed—what else could he do? He had been accustomed to doing this when he was in trouble.

"I cried by reason of mine affliction unto the Lord, and He heard me; out of the belly of hell cried I, and Thou heardst my voice. . . .And the Lord spake unto the fish, and it vomited out Jonah upon the dry land" (Jonah 2:2,10).

Like others, he joined prayer to a vow he had made, as he says in his prayer, "But I will sacrifice unto Thee with the voice of thanksgiving; I will pay *that* that I have vowed. Salvation is of the Lord" (Jonah 2:9).

Prayer was the mighty force which brought Jonah from "the belly of hell." Prayer, mighty prayer, secured the end. Prayer brought God to the rescue of unfaithful Jonah, despite his sin of fleeing from duty. God could not deny his prayer. Nothing is beyond the reach of prayer because no prayer is too hard for God to answer.

The mighty results of Jonah's prayer became an Old Testament type of the miraculous power displayed in the resurrection from the dead of Jesus Christ.

Believe God Hears Your Prayer

Through these stories, the Bible clearly points out that prayer is only significant because God hears and answers it. The Old Testament saints strongly believed this fact. The belief that God would answer prayer is the one characteristic that stands out prominently and continuously in their lives. They were essentially men of prayer.

How we need a school to teach the art of praying! Prayer, the simplest of all arts and mightiest of all forces, is always in danger of being forgotten or corrupted. As we grow older, worldy influences constantly attempt to break down our childhood prayer lessons. Old Testament people however, because of their simpler culture, had less difficulty praying. These men and women had a childlike faith in God.

In citing Old Testament saints noted for their praying habits, David must not be overlooked. David is the most noted of Old Testament saints for his communication with God in prayer. Prayer was a habit to him. We hear him say, "Evening, and morning, and at noon, will I pray, and cry aloud" (Psalm 55:17). Prayer for the gentle Psalmist of Israel was no strange occupation. He knew the way to God and was often found in fellowship with Him.

It is no wonder we hear his clear and impressive call, "O come, let us worship and bow down: let us kneel before the Lord our maker" (Psalm 95:6). He knew God was the one being who could answer prayer: "O Thou that hearest prayer, unto Thee shall all flesh come" (Psalm 65:2).

When God struck down Bathsheba's child because David's grievous sins gave God's enemies an opportunity to blaspheme, it is no surprise that David spent an entire week praying and fasting for his child's recovery. God's denial of his request, however, did not affect David's habit of praying or his faith in God. While God did not give David the life of this son, He later gave David another son named Solomon.

In close connection with this season of prayer was David's penitential praying. Nathan, by God's command, uncovered David's two great sins of adultery and murder. David immediately acknowledged his wickedness saying to Nathan, "I have sinned" (2 Samuel 12:13). Psalm 51 is his heart's cry of deep grief and genuine repentance.

David knew where to find God, who would pardon his sins. God received him back, and he had the joys of salvation restored to him by earnest, sincere, penitential praying. In the same way, God answers all sinners' repentant prayers and brings them back into divine favor, pardoning them and giving them a new heart.

The entire book of Psalms brings prayer to the forefront showing how personal communication with God can bristle with life and feeling.

God's Abundant Answers

Solomon must not be overlooked either in the catalog of Old Testament praying men. While in his later life Solomon departed from God, he often prayed at the beginning of his reign. On one occasion, Solomon went to Gibeon to offer a sacrifice. While offering the sacrifice, Solomon prayed. That night the Lord appeared to Solomon in a vision saying, "Ask what I shall give thee" (1 Kings 3:5). The following account of his request shows the quality of Solomon's character.

"O Lord my God, Thou hast made Thy servant king instead of David my father: and I am but a little child: I know not how to go out or to come in.

"And Thy servant is in the midst of Thy people which Thou hast chosen, a great people, that cannot be numbered nor counted for multitude.

"Give therefore Thy servant an understanding heart to judge Thy people, that I may discern between good and bad: for who is able to judge this Thy so great a people?" (1 Kings 3:7-9).

No wonder that, as a result of such praying, the Lord responded in a generous and powerful way.

"And the speech pleased the Lord, that Solomon had asked this thing.

"And God said unto him, Because thou hast asked this thing, and hast not asked for thyself long life; neither hast asked riches for thyself, nor hast asked the life of thine enemies; but hast asked for thyself understanding to discern judgment;

"Behold, I have done according to thy words: lo, I have given thee a wise and an understanding heart; so that there was none like thee before thee, neither after thee shall any arise like unto thee.

"And I have also given thee that which thou hast not asked, both riches, and honour: so that there shall not be any among the kings like unto thee all thy days" (1 Kings 3:10-13).

What powerful prayer! What self-deprecation and simplicity! "I am but a little child" (1 Kings 3:7). He really specified what he needed! Because of his attitude, God answered with more than what Solomon asked!

The remarkable prayer at the dedication of the temple is another example. This could be the longest recorded prayer in God's Word. How comprehensive, direct, and intense it was! Solomon could not afford to lay the foundation of God's house without prayer. God heard this prayer as He heard them before, "the glory of the Lord filled the house" (1 Kings 8:11). Thus God confirmed acceptance of this house of worship and of Solomon, the praying king.

The list of Old Testament saints who were devoted to prayer is too long to discuss at length. However, as the Scripture reader examines other praying men of God, he will want to include Isaiah and Jeremiah. Careful readers will see how great a place prayer occupied in the minds and lives of the men of those early days.

Chapter 3

BEGINNING WITH PRAYER

"Oh, for determined men and women, who will rise early and really burn out for God. Oh, for a faith that will sweep into heaven with the early dawn and have ships from a shoreless sea loaded in the soul's harbor ere the ordinary laborer has knocked the dew from his scythe or the peddler has turned from his pallet of straw to spread nature's treasures of fruit before the early buyers"—Rev. Homer W. Hodge.

Prayer reaches back to man's first existence on earth. We see how the energy of prayer is required in the simplest as well as the most complex provision of God's grace.

Abraham, the friend of God, is a striking illustration of one of the Old Testament saints who strongly believed in prayer. Abraham was not by any means a shadowy figure. God called Abraham to journey to an unknown land taking his entire household. Whenever Abraham stopped for the night or longer, he always erected an altar and "called on the name of the Lord" (Genesis 13:4).

This man of faith and prayer was one of the first to erect a family altar, around which he gathered his household and offered sacrifices of worship, praise, and prayer. Abraham's altars were essentially altars where he gathered his household, as distinguished from secret prayer.

Blessing And Power Through Prayer

As God's revelations became fuller, Abraham's prayerfulness increased, and it was during one of these spiritual meetings that "Abraham fell on his face: and God talked with him" (Genesis 17:3). On still another occasion, we find this man, "the father of the faithful," praying on his face before God, astonished at the answers, purposes, and revelations of Almighty God for him. God was promising him a son in his old age as well as great honor for this son.

Even Ishmael's destiny was shaped by Abraham's prayer when he prayed, "O that Ishmael might live before Thee!" (Genesis 17:18).

What a remarkable story of Abraham's standing before God repeating his intercessions for the wicked city of Sodom. Sodom was the home of his nephew, Lot, and was doomed by God's decision to destroy it! Sodom's fate was delayed for a while by Abraham's praying, and it was almost entirely relieved by the humility and insistence of his prayers. Abraham believed strongly in prayer and knew how to pray. No other recourse was open to Abraham to save Sodom but prayer.

Perhaps the failure to ultimately rescue Sodom

from her doom of destruction was due to Abraham's optimistic view of the spiritual condition of things in that city. Perhaps if Abraham had entreated God once more, asking Him to spare the city even if He found only one righteous man for Lot's sake, God might have heeded Abraham's request.

Another instance in the life of Abraham shows how he was a man of prayer and had power with God. Abraham had journeyed to and was lodging in Gerar. Fearing that Abimelech might kill him and appropriate Sarah his wife for his own lustful uses, he deceived Abimelech by claiming Sarah was his sister. God appeared unto Abimelech in a dream and warned him not to touch Sarah, telling him that she was Abraham's wife, not his sister. He said unto Abimelech, "Now therefore restore the man his wife; for he is a prophet, and he shall pray for thee, and thou shalt live" (Genesis 20:7).

The conclusion of the incident is recorded in Genesis 20:17-18: "So Abraham prayed unto God: and God healed Abimelech and his wife, and his maid servants; and they bare children. For the Lord had fast closed up all the wombs of the house of Abimelech because of Sarah, Abraham's wife."

This case is similar to that of Job's at the close of his fearful experience and terrible trials. His friends, neither understanding him nor comprehending God's dealings with His servant, falsely charged Job with being in sin. They cited this presumed sin as the cause of his troubles. God said to Job's friends, "My servant Job shall pray for you:

for him will I accept. . . .And the Lord turned the captivity of Job, when he prayed for his friends" (Job 42:8,10).

Almighty God knew His servant Job as a man of prayer, and He could afford to send Job's friends to him for prayer in order to carry out and fulfill His plans and purposes.

It was Abraham's rule to stand before the Lord in prayer. His life was surcharged with prayer, and Abraham's blessing was sanctified by prayer. Wherever he halted in his pilgrimage, he always asked for God's blessing through prayer. Side by side with the sacrifice altar was the prayer altar. He arose early in the morning and went to stand before the Lord in prayer.

Chapter 4

INTERCESSORY PRAYER MOVES GOD

"Intercessory prayer is a powerful means of grace for the praying man. The English missionary Martyn observes that at times of inward dryness and depression, he often found a delightful revival in the act of praying for others, for their conversion, or sanctification, or prosperity in the work of the Lord. His intercession with God about these gifts and blessings were, for himself, the divinely natural channel of a renewed insight into his own part and lot in Christ. Christ was his own rest and power, into the 'perfect freedom' of an entire yielding of himself to his Master for His work"—Bishop Handley C.G. Moule.

Prayer unites with God's purposes and lays itself out to secure those purposes. How often would the wise and benign will of God fail in its rich and beneficent ends by the sins of the people if prayer had not come in to arrest wrath and make the promise sure! Israel as a nation would have met their just destruction after their apostasy with the golden calf had it not been for the unfainting intercession of Moses' forty days and forty nights of praying!

Moses' character was greatly affected by his praying. His forty days of close interaction in prayer with God worked a greater character transfiguration than his exchanges with God when he received the law. When he came down from the mountain after his long prayer, his face shone with dazzling brightness. Our heights of transfiguration and loving character and conduct are born of seasons of prayer. Through all-night praying God has responded by changing many a Jacob, a supplanter, into an Israel, a prince, who has power with God and men.

No mission was more majestic in purpose and results than that of Moses. None was more responsible, diligent, or difficult. His mission teaches us the noble ministry of prayer. Not only is prayer the medium of supply and support, but it is a compassionate agency through which the pitying, long-suffering God has an outflow. Prayer is a medium to restrain God's wrath, allowing mercy to rejoice against judgment.

Moses himself and his mission were the answer to prayer. 1 Samuel 12:8 records, "When Jacob was come into Egypt, and your fathers cried unto the Lord, then the Lord sent Moses and Aaron, which brought forth your fathers out of Egypt, and made them dwell in this place." This was the beginning of the great deliverance of the Hebrews from Egyptian bondage.

The great movements of God originated with and were shaped by prayers of men. Prayer deals directly with God. He is pleased to order His policy and base His action on the prayers of His saints. Prayer influences God greatly. Moses could not do God's great work, even though it was God-commissioned, without praying. Moses could not govern God's people and carry out the divine plans without having his censer full of the incense of prayer. The work of God cannot be done unless the fire and fragrance of prayer are always burning, ascending, and perfuming.

Deal With God Directly

Moses prayed often to relieve the terrible stroke of God's wrath. Four times Pharaoh solicited the prayers of Moses for relief from the fearful blow of God's wrath. "Intreat the Lord" (Exodus 8:8), begged Pharaoh while the loathsome frogs were upon him. And "Moses cried unto the Lord because of the frogs which He had brought against Pharaoh. And the Lord did according to the words of Moses" (Exodus 8:12-13). God answered his prayers.

When the grievous plague of flies had corrupted the whole land, Pharaoh again piteously cried out to Moses, "Intreat for me" (Exodus 8:28). Moses left Pharaoh and begged the Lord, and again the Lord answered and did as Moses asked.

The plague of fiery hail, which destroyed all of Egypt's crops, brought Pharaoh to Moses with the same earnest appeal, "Intreat the Lord" (Exodus

9:28). Moses went into the privacy of the wilderness alone with Almighty God. He "spread abroad his hands unto the Lord: and the thunders and hail ceased, and the rain was not poured upon the earth" (Exodus 9:33).

Though Moses was the man of law, prayer with him still asserted its mighty force. As in the more spiritual dispensation, Moses could have said, "My house is the house of prayer" (Luke 19:46). Moses accepted the foundation principle of praying at its full face value.

Prayer deals directly with God. With Abraham we saw this clearly and strongly enunciated. With Moses it is still clearer and stronger, if possible. The principle is: prayer affects God. God's conduct is influenced by prayer. A continuation of this principle is that God hears and answers prayer even when the hearing and answering might change His conduct and reverse His action. The decree, "Call unto Me and I will answer thee" (Jeremiah 33:3), is stronger than all other laws and more inflexible than any other decree.

Moses had a bold, free, and unhindered access to God. Familiarity and closeness to God gives prayer delight, frequency, focus, and potency. Those who know God the best are the richest and most powerful in obtaining answers to prayer. Prayer becomes a rare thing for those unacquainted with God.

Moses sometimes found himself reduced to extreme conditions which God decided not to relieve. However, there are no circumstances too extreme for God to relieve.

Moses' mission was divine. It was ordered, directed, and planned by God. The more there is of God in a movement, the more prayer is conspicuous. Moses urgently prayed for the salvation of the Lord's people for forty days and forty nights. His concern was so intense for them that his physical infirmities and appetites were taken away during long seasons of prayer.

Evidence of the strange effect a righteous man's prayers have on God can be seen in God's exclamation to Moses, "Now, therefore, let Me alone, that My wrath may wax hot against them, that I may consume them; and I will make of thee a great nation" (Deuteronomy 9:14). The presence of such an influence over God fills us with astonishment, awe, and fear. How bold, lofty, and devoted is such a pleader!

Moses' Intercessory Prayers

Read this from the divine record:

"And Moses returned unto the Lord, and said, Oh, this people have sinned a great sin, and have made them gods of gold.

"Yet now, if Thou wilt forgive their sin—and if not, blot me, I pray Thee, out of Thy books which Thou hast written.

"And the Lord said unto Moses, Whosoever hath sinned against Me, him will I blot out of My book.

"Therefore now go, lead the people unto the place of which I have spoken unto thee: Behold Mine Angel shall go before thee" (Exodus 32:31-

35).

At the rebellion of Korah, God's anger flamed out against everyone in Israel who sympathized with these rebels. Again Moses appeared on the stage of action, this time Aaron joined him in intercession for these sinners. It shows that in a serious time like this Moses knew where to go for relief. He knew to pray that God would answer by holding back His wrath to spare Israel. Here is what Scripture says about the situation:

"And the Lord spake unto Moses and unto Aaron, saying,

"Separate yourselves from among this congregation, that I may consume them in a moment.

"And they fell on their faces, and said, O God, the God of the spirits of all flesh, shall one man sin, and wilt Thou be wroth with all the congregation?" (Numbers 16:20-22).

The assumption, pride, and rebellion of Miriam, sister of Moses, in which she had the presence and sympathy of Aaron, put the praying and the spirit of Moses in the noblest and most amiable light. Because of her sin, God smote her with leprosy. But Moses made tender and earnest intercession for his sister who had so grievously offended God. His prayer was answered, and God saved her from the fearful and incurable malady.

The record is very interesting.

"And the anger of the Lord was kindled against them; and He departed. And the cloud departed from off the tabernacle; and behold, Miriam became leprous, white as snow: and Aaron looked

31

upon Miriam, and, behold, she was leprous.

"And Aaron said unto Moses, Alas, my lord, I beseech thee, lay not the sin upon us, wherein we have done foolishly, and wherein we have sinned.

"Let her not be as one dead, of whom the flesh is half consumed when he cometh out of his mother's womb.

"And Moses cried unto the Lord, saying, Heal her now, O God, I beseech Thee.

"And the Lord said unto Moses, If her father had but spit in her face, should she not be ashamed seven days? Let her be shut out from the camp seven days, and after that let her be received again" (Numbers 12:9-14).

The murmurings of the children of Israel furnished conditions which called into play the full force of prayer. These conditions impressively bring out the intercessory feature of prayer and disclose Moses in his great office as an intercessor. It was at Marah that the waters were bitter, and it was here that the people grievously murmured against Moses and God.

Here is the Scripture account:

"And when they came to Marah, they could not drink of the waters of Marah, for they were bitter: therefore the name of it was called Marah.

"And the people murmured against Moses, saying, What shall we drink?

"And he cried unto the Lord; and the Lord shewed him a tree, which when he had cast into the waters, the waters were made sweet: there he made for them a statute and an ordinance, and there he proved them'' (Exodus 15:25).

The records of eternity alone will disclose how many bitter places of the earth have been sweetened by answers to prayer.

Again at Taberah the people complained, and God became angry with them. Moses again came to the front, stepped into the breach, and prayed for them. Here is the brief account:

"And when the people complained, it displeased the Lord: and the Lord heard it; and His anger was kindled; and the fire of the Lord burnt among them, and consumed them that were in the uttermost part of the camp.

"And the people cried unto Moses, and when Moses prayed unto the Lord, the fire was quenched" (Numbers 11:1-2).

Grace For Everyday Living

Moses got what he asked for. His praying was specific, and God's answer was likewise specific. Almighty God always heard Moses when he prayed and always answered. Once the answer was not specific. He prayed to go into Canaan. The answer came, but it was not what he asked for. He was given a vision of the Promised Land, but he was not allowed to cross the Jordan into that land.

It was a prayer on the order of Paul's when he prayed three times for the removal of the thorn in the flesh. The thorn, however, was not removed. God did provide grace which made the thorn a blessing.

The ninetieth Psalm, though it is incorporated

with the "Psalms of David," is attributed to Moses. It gives us a prayer sample of God's lawgiver. It is a prayer worth studying. It is sacred because it has been the requiem uttered over our dead for years. However, its very familiarity may cause us to lose its full meaning.

We would be wise if we digested it, not for the dead, but for the living, and let it teach us how to live, how to pray while living, and how to die. "So teach us to number our days, that we may apply our hearts to wisdom. . . .Establish Thou the work of our hands upon us; yea, the work of our hands establish Thou it" (Psalm 90:12,17).

Chapter 5

PRAYER, THE PROPHET'S LINK TO GOD

" 'I have known men,' says Goodwin, 'who came to God for other reasons than to come to Him, they so loved Him. They refused to soil either Him or themselves with any other purpose than to simply be alone with Him. Friendship is best kept up, even among men, by frequent visits; and the more free from impurity those frequent visits are, and the less brought about by business, necessity, or custom, the more friendly and welcome they are' "—Rev. Alexander Whyte.

Elijah is the preeminent elder of the prophets. The crown, the throne and the scepter are his. His garments are white with flame. He seems exalted in his fiery and prayerful nature, like a superhuman being. But the New Testament places him alongside us as a man with a similar nature to ours. Instead of placing himself outside the sphere of humanity, in the marvelous fruit of his praying, Scripture points to him as an example to be imitated and as inspiration to stimulate us. To pray and have results like Elijah is the crying need of our times.

Elijah learned the lesson of prayer, and he graduated from that divine school before Scripture mentions him. Somewhere in the secret places, on a mountain or a plain, he had been alone with God as an intercessor against the debasing idolatry of Ahab. His prayers prevailed mightily with God. He was certain that his prayers were answered.

He had been talking with God about vengeance. He was the embodiment of his times—times of vengeance. The intercessor was not to be clothed with an olive branch—the symbol of a suppliant for mercy—but with fire—the symbol of justice and the messenger of wrath. Self-assured and with holy boldness, he declared to the astonished, cowering king his fearful message—a message gained by his earnest praying—and God did not deny his prayer. "As the Lord God of Israel liveth, before whom I stand, there shall not be dew nor rain these years, but according to my word" (1 Kings 17:1).

Resistless Prayer

The secret of his praying and his close relationship with God are found in the words, "Before whom I stand." Gabriel's words to Zacharias informing this priest of his coming are similar: "I am Gabriel that standeth in the presence of God" (Luke 1:19). The archangel Gabriel had just a little more unflinching devotion, courage, readiness of obedience, and zeal for God's honor than Elijah.

What answers to prayer! What lasting power was

in his prayer! "And it rained not on earth by the space of three years and six months" (James 5:17). What a man who dared utter such a claim and assert such power! Elijah's praying was no mere sham or performance, no spiritless, soulless, official praying. Elijah was in Elijah's praying. The whole man, with all his fiery forces, prayed unceasingly. Almighty God was real to him. Prayer to him was the means of projecting God in full force on the world, in order to vindicate His name, establish His own being, avenge His blasphemed name and violated law, and vindicate His servants.

Instead of "prayed earnestly," in James 5:17, the Revised Standard Version has it, "In his prayer he prayed" or "with prayer he prayed." That is, he prayed with all the combined energies of prayer.

Elijah's praying was strong, insistent, and resistless in its elements of power. Feeble praying secures no results and brings neither glory to God nor good to man.

Provision For A Widow

Elijah learned new and higher lessons of prayer with God while hidden away by the brook, Cherith. He was doubtless communing with God while Ahab was searching everywhere for him. After a while God ordered him to Sarepta, where He had commanded a widow to sustain Elijah.

He went there for the widow's good as well as for his own. While this woman provided for him, he provided for the woman. Elijah's prayers did more for the woman than the woman's hospitality did for Elijah. Great trials and sorrows awaited the widow yet, great answers, too. Her widowhood and her poverty tell of her struggles and her sorrows. Elijah was there to relieve her poverty and to assuage her griefs.

Here is the interesting account:

"And it came to pass after these things, that the son of the woman, the mistress of the house, fell sick; and his sickness was so sore, that there was no breath left in him.

"And she said unto Elijah, What have I do to with with thee, O thou man of God? art thou come unto me to call my sin to remembrance, and to slay my son?

"And he said unto her, Give me thy son. And he took him out of her bosom, and carried him up into a loft, where he abode, and laid him down upon his own bed.

"And he cried unto the Lord, and said, O Lord my God, hast Thou also brought evil upon the widow with whom I sojourn, by slaying her son?

"And he stretched himself upon the child three times, and cried unto the Lord, and said, O Lord my God, I pray Thee, let this child's soul come into him again.

"And the Lord heard the voice of Elijah; and the soul of the child came into him again, and he revived.

"And Elijah took the child and brought him down out of the chamber into the house, and delivered him unto his mother: and Elijah said, See, thy son liveth.

"And the woman said to Elijah, Now by this I know that thou art a man of God, and that the word of the Lord in thy mouth is truth" (1 Kings 17:17-24).

Elijah's prayer entered a region where prayer had never gone before. The awful, mysterious, and powerful regions of the dead were invaded by the presence and demands of prayer. God's answers to Elijah's praying kept the woman from starving and brought her son back from death. Surely no sorrow is like the bitterness of the loss of an only son.

Elijah faced these conditions full of confidence. There was no hesitancy in his actions, and there was no pause in his faith. He took the dead son to his own room, and alone with God he prayed. In that room, God met him. The encounter was too intense and too sacred for a third party to share.

The prayer was made to God, and the issue was with God. God took the child, and only God rules the realms of death. In His hands are the issues of life and death. Elijah believed that God took the child's spirit, and that God could also restore that spirit.

God answered Elijah's prayer. The answer was proof of Elijah's mission and the truth of God's Word. The dead child brought to life was a sure conviction of this truth: "Now by this I know that thou art a man of God, and that the word of the Lord in thy mouth is truth" (1 Kings 17:24). Answers to prayer are evidences of God and the truth of His Word.

Elijah's Noteworthy Prayer

The unforgettable test of Elijah, made in the presence of an apostate king, in the face of a backslidden nation ruled by an idolatrous priesthood, is a sublime exhibition of faith and prayer. The prophets of Baal lost the contest. No fire from heaven fell in answer to their frantic cries.

Elijah, in great quietness of spirit and with confident assurance, called Israel to him. He repaired the wasted altar of God, the altar of sacrifice and of prayer, and put the pieces of bullock in order on the altar. He then took action to prevent any charge of deception. He flooded the altar with water. Then Elijah prayed a model prayer, remarkable for its clarity, simplicity, and candor. It is also noted for its brevity and faith.

Read the account given in Scripture:

"And it came to pass at the time of the offering of the evening sacrifice, that Elijah the prophet came near, and said, Lord God of Abraham, Isaac, and of Israel, let it be known this day that Thou art God in Israel, and that I am Thy servant, and that I have done all these things at Thy word.

"Hear me, O Lord, hear me, that this people may know that Thou art the Lord God, and that Thou hast turned their heart back again.

"Then the fire of the Lord fell, and consumed the burnt sacrifice, and the wood, and the stones, and the dust, and licked up the water that was in the trench.

"And when all the people saw it, they fell on

their faces: and they said, The Lord, He is the God; The Lord, He is the God" (1 Kings 18:36-39).

Elijah was dealing directly with God as before. True prayer always deals directly with God. Elijah's prayer was to determine the existence of the true God. The answer, direct from God, settled the question. The answer is also the proof of Elijah's divine mission and the evidence that God deals with men. If we had more of Elijah's praying, marvels would be greater than those things we call marvels today. God would not seem so strange, so far away, and so feeble in action. Everything is tame and feeble to us because our praying is so tame and feeble.

Fiery Praying Brings Rain

God said to Elijah, "Go shew thyself unto Ahab; and I will send rain on the earth" (1 Kings 18:1). Elijah acted promptly on the divine order and showed himself to Ahab. He made his issue with Ahab, Israel, and Baal. The whole current of national feeling turned back to God. The day faded into the evening shades. No rain had come. But Elijah did not fold his arms and say the promise had failed. He emphasized the promise and saw God fulfill it.

Here is the Scripture record with the result given:

"And Elijah said unto Ahab, Get thee up, eat and drink; for there is a sound of abundance of rain.

"So Ahab went up to eat and to drink. And Elijah went up to the top of Carmel; and he cast himself

41

down upon the earth, and put his face between his knees.

"And said to his servant, Go up now, look toward the sea. And he went up, and looked, and said, There is nothing. And he said, Go again seven times.

"And it came to pass at the seventh time, that he said, Behold, there riseth a little cloud out of the sea, like a man's hand. And he said, Go up say unto Ahab, Prepare thy chariot, and get thee down, that the rain stop thee not.

"And it came to pass in the mean while, that the heaven was black with clouds and wind, and there was a great rain. And Ahab rode, and went to Jezreel.

"And the hand of the Lord was on Elijah" (1 Kings 18:41-46).

Then it was, as James records, "And he prayed again, and the heaven gave rain, and the earth brought forth her fruit" (James 5:18).

Elijah's persistent, fiery praying and God's promise brought the rain. Prayer carries the promise to its gracious fulfillment. It takes persistent and persevering prayer to give the promise its largest and most gracious results. In this instance, it was expectant prayer, watchful of results, looking for the answer. Elijah's answer was the small cloud like a man's hand. He had the inward assurance of the answer even before he had the rain.

Elijah's praying shames our feeble praying! His praying made things happen. It vindicated God's existence, brought conviction to dull and sluggish consciences, and proved that God was still Master of the nation. Elijah's praying turned a whole nation back to God, ordered the moving of the clouds, and directed the falling of the rain. It called down fire from heaven to prove God's existence or destroy His enemies.

Mighty In Prayer, Mighty With God

The Elder Prophet of Israel's praying was clothed in fire. He wore a golden crown, and his censer was full of burning, fragrant prayer. No wonder Elisha cried out as he saw the fiery prophet of the Lord enter the chariot for his heavenly ride, "My father, my father, the chariot of Israel, and the horsemen thereof" (2 Kings 2:12). But chariots and armies could not begin to do as much for Israel as the praying Elijah. Elijah could not touch anything except through prayer. God was with him mightily because he was mighty in prayer.

Today we need saints who dare to pray with the fire, force, and fragrance of Elijah's prayers!

In the contest with the prophets of Baal, the issue is clearly to determine the true God. Does God live? Is the Bible a revelation from Him? How often do those questions arise? How often do they need to be settled? An appeal by prayer is the only way to settle them. The trouble is not in God, but in our praying. The proof that God exists are His answered prayers.

Where are the Elijah's in today's Church? Where are the men with his fervor, who can pray as he prayed? We have thousands of intense men, but where are the men who will pray as he prayed? Notice the calm, assured confidence he displayed as he staked the issue and built the altar. His prayer was clear and calm on that occasion.

Elijah's praying follows New Testament prayer principles and illustrates the nature of prayer. It also proves what prayer can do for the person who prays with confidence and faith. Elijah's results could be secured today if we had more Elijah men praying.

Elijah obtained his answers by praying truly and earnestly. So much of today's praying is not real praying, but a mere shell, mere words! Most of it could be called non-praying. It goes nowhere and accomplishes nothing. In fact, very often no results are even expected.

True prayer that wins an answer must be backed up by a scriptural, vital, personal religion. They are the essentials of real Christian service in this life. Of these requirements the most important is that in serving, we serve. So in praying, we must talk with God. Truth and heart reality, these are the core, the substance, the sum, the heart of prayer. Prayer has no potential unless we pray with simplicity, sincerity, and truth. Prayerless praying—how popular, yet what a useless delusion!

Chapter 6

EVEN KINGS MUST PRAY

"One can form a habit of study until the will seems to be at rest and only the intellect is engaged, the will having retired altogether from exercise. This is not true of real praying. If the affections are laggard, cold, indifferent, if the intellect is furnishing no material to clothe the petition then nothing worthwhile is accomplished"—Rev. Homer W. Hodge.

The great religious reformation under King Hezekiah and the prophet Isaiah was thoroughly saturated with prayer during various stages. King Hezekiah serves as an illustration of a praying elder of Israel, white-robed and gold-crowned. He had genius and strength, wisdom and piety. He was a statesman, a general, a poet, and a religious reformer. He surprises us, not so much because of his strength and genius—they were to be expected—but because of his piety under all the circumstances connected with him.

The rare statement, "He did that which was right in the sight of the Lord" (2 Chronicles

29:2), is a thrilling surprise when we consider all his antecedents and his environments. Where did he come from? Under what circumstances was his childhood spent? Who were his parents and what was their religious character?

Worldliness, half-heartedness, and utter apostasy marked the reign of his father, grandfather, and his great-grandfather. As he grew up, his home surroundings were far from being a foundation for godliness and faith in God. One thing, however, favored him. He was fortunate to have Isaiah for his friend and counselor when he assumed the crown of Judah. It is extremely valuable for a ruler to have a God-fearing man for his counselor and associate!

Law Yielded To Prayer

Hezekiah interceded on behalf of a number of people who were unfit to participate in the Passover feast. These people were not prepared with the required ceremonial cleansing, and it was important that they be allowed to eat the Passover feast with everyone.

Here is the brief account, with special reference to Hezekiah's praying and God's response:

"For there were many in the congregation that were not sanctified: therefore the Levites had the charge of the killing of the passover for every one that was not clean, to sanctify them unto the Lord.

"For a multitude of the people, had not cleansed themselves, yet did they eat the passover otherwise than it was written. But Hezekiah prayed for them, saying, The good Lord pardon every one that prepareth his heart to seek God, the Lord God of his fathers, though he be not cleansed according to the purification of the sanctuary.

"And the Lord hearkened to Hezekiah, and healed the people" (2 Chronicles 30:17-20).

So the Lord heard his prayer and even the violation of the most sacred law of the Passover was forgiven to answer this praying, God-fearing king. Law must yield its scepter to prayer.

The strength, directness, and foundation of Hezekiah's faith and prayer are found in his words to his army. They are memorable words, stronger and mightier than all the armies of Sennacherib:

"Be strong and courageous, be not afraid nor dismayed for the king of Assyria, nor for all the multitude that is with him, for there be more with us than with him.

"With him is an arm of flesh; but with us is the Lord our God to help us, and to fight our battles. And the people rested themselves upon the words of Hezekiah king of Judah" (2 Chronicles 32:7-8).

Turn To God First

Hezekiah's defense against the mighty enemies of God was prayer. His enemies cowered and were destroyed by God's answers to his prayers even when his own armies were powerless. God's people were always safe when their princes were princes in prayer.

One momentous occasion really tested Hezekiah's faith, furnishing him with an opportunity to try prayer as a means to deliverance. Judah was sorely pressed by the Assyrians, and, humanly speaking, defeat and captivity seemed imminent. The king of Assyria sent a commission to defy and blaspheme the name of God and to insult King Hezekiah publicly. Note what Hezekiah did without hesitation: "And it came to pass when King Hezekiah heard it, that he rent his clothes and covered himself with sackcloth, and went into the house of the Lord" (Isaiah 37:1).

His very first reflex was to turn to God by entering the "house of prayer." God was in his thoughts, and prayer was the first action to be taken. He sent messengers to Isaiah asking Isaiah to join him in prayer. Isaiah and Hezekiah appealed to God for deliverance from these blasphemous enemies.

Just at this particular point in time, the Assyrian king's forces, which were besieging Hezekiah, were diverted from an immediate attack on Jerusalem. This was God's answer. The king of Assyria, however, sent Hezekiah a defaming and blasphemous letter.

The second time he was surrounded by the forces of this heathen king, Hezekiah entered the Lord's house, the house of prayer. He knew exactly where he should go and to whom he should appeal.

"And Hezekiah received the letter from the hand of the messengers, and read it: and Hezekiah went up unto the house of the Lord, and spread it before the Lord.

"And Hezekiah prayed unto the Lord, saying, O Lord of hosts, God of Israel, that dwellest between the cherubims, Thou art the God, even Thou alone, of all the kingdoms of the earth: Thou hast made heaven and earth.

"Now therefore, O Lord our God, save us from his hand, that all the kingdoms of the earth may know that Thou art the Lord, even Thou only" (Isaiah 37:14-16,20).

God Upholds His Honor

Note the speedy answer and the marvelous results of such praying by this God-fearing king. First, Isaiah gave the king full assurance that he need fear nothing. God heard the prayer and would give a great deliverance.

Secondly, the angel of the Lord came with swift wings and smote 185,000 Assyrians. The king was vindicated, God was honored, and the people of God were saved.

The united prayers of the praying king and the praying prophet were mighty forces in bringing God's deliverance and destroying His enemies. Armies were at their mercy. Angels, swift-winged and armed with almighty power and vengeance, were their allies.

Hezekiah served his people in prayer to destroy idolatry and reform his kingdom. Prayer was his chief weapon. He later tried its power against the set and declared plan of Almighty God. When Hezekiah was very sick, God sent his close friend, wise counselor, and prophet, Isaiah, to warn him of his approaching end. Isaiah also told him to arrange his affairs in preparation for his final departure. This is the scriptural statement: "In those days was Hezekiah sick unto death. And the Prophet Isaiah the son of Amoz came to him, and said unto him, Thus saith the Lord, Set thine house in order; for thou shalt die, and not live" (2 Kings 20:1).

The decree came directly from God. He wondered what could reverse that divine decree. Hezekiah had never been in a situation so insurmountable, with a decree so direct and definite from God. Could prayer change the purposes of God? Could prayer snatch from the jaws of death one who was destined to die? Could prayer save a man from an incurable sickness? These were the questions with which he had to deal.

But his faith did not waver one moment. His faith did not stagger one minute when the Lord's prophet suddenly gave him the definite news. Hezekiah did not let any untrusting, unbelieving thoughts enter his mind—as believers might today. Instantly he started to pray. Immediately, without delay, he petitioned God who issued the edict. He could not go to anyone else. God could change His own purposes if He so chose.

Note what Hezekiah did in this emergency and the gracious result.

"Then he turned his face to the wall, and prayed unto the Lord, saying, I beseech Thee, O Lord, remember now how I have walked before Thee in truth and with a perfect heart, and have done that which is good in Thy sight. And Hezekiah wept sore'' (2 Kings 20:2-3).

He did not offer God a self-righteous plea for recovery. He wanted God to remember his sincerity, fidelity, and service—which was legitimate. This prayer was directly in line with that of David in Psalm 26:1, "Judge me, O Lord; for I have walked in mine integrity." This was not a prayer test with Hezekiah, nor was it a faith cure, but it was testing God. It had to be God's cure if a cure was to come at all.

Tears Bring Answers

Hezekiah hardly finished his prayer, and Isaiah was just about to go home, when God gave another message for Hezekiah. This time the message was more pleasant and encouraging. The mighty force of prayer had affected God and had changed His edict reversing His purpose concerning Hezekiah. Prayer can accomplish anything. A praying man can accomplish anything through prayer.

"And it came to pass afore Isaiah was gone out into the middle court, that the word of the Lord came to him, saying,

"Turn again, and tell Hezekiah the captain of My people, Thus saith the Lord, the God of David thy father, I have heard thy prayer, I have seen thy tears: behold, I will heal thee: on the third day thou shalt go up unto the house of the Lord.

"And I will add unto thy days fifteen years; and I will deliver thee and this city out of the hand of the king of Assyria; and I will defend this city for

Mine own sake, and for My servant David's sake''
(2 Kings 20:4-6).

The prayer was to God. It asked God to recon-
sider and change His mind. Doubtless Isaiah
returned to his house with a lighter heart than
when he delivered his original message. This sick
king prayed to God, asking Him to revoke His
decree, and God condescended to grant the
request. God sometimes changes His mind in
answer to prayer. He has a right to do so. His
reasons for changing His mind are strong reasons.
His servant Hezekiah wanted it done.

Hezekiah had been a dutiful servant for God.
Truth, perfection, and goodness were the elements of Hezekiah's service and the rule of his
life. Hezekiah's tears and prayer were in the way
of God's executing His decree to take away His
servant's life. Prayer and tears are mighty things
with God. They mean much more to Him than
consistency and decrees. ''I have heard thy prayer,
I have seen thy tears: behold, I will heal thee'' (2
Kings 20:5).

Health comes in answer to prayer. God
answered by giving more than what Hezekiah
asked. Hezekiah prayed only for his life. God not
only gave him life, but He also promised him protection and security from his enemies.

Isaiah also had something to do with the recovery of this praying king. Isaiah's praying was
changed into the skill of the physician. ''And
Isaiah said, Take a lump of figs. And they took and
laid it on the boil, and he recovered'' (2 Kings

20:7).

Isaiah and Hezekiah prayed further for concrete proof of God's healing.

"And Hezekiah said unto Isaiah, What shall be the sign that the Lord will heal me, and that I shall go up into the house of the Lord the third day?

"And Isaiah said, This sign shalt thou have of the Lord, that the Lord will do the thing that He hath spoken: shall the shadow go forward ten degrees, or go back ten degrees?

"And Hezekiah answered, It is a light thing for the shadow to go down ten degrees: nay, but let the shadow return backward ten degrees.

"And Isaiah the prophet cried unto the Lord: and he brought the shadow ten degrees backward, by which it had gone down in the dial of Ahaz" (2 Kings 20:8-11).

Life was sweet to Hezekiah, and he wanted to live. Nothing but the energy of faith could have impelled God to act so powerfully. Hezekiah's heart was broken, and his tears added force and volume to his prayer. He pleaded with great strivings and strong arguments. God heard Hezekiah praying, saw his tears, and changed His mind.

Hezekiah lived to praise God and be an example of God's answers to mighty praying. His prayer was born in the fire of great desire, and it pursued through the deepest agony of conflict and opposition to find success.

Spiritual cravings must be strong enough to give life to the mighty conflicts of prayer. They must be absorbing enough to stop business, arrest worldly pursuits, awaken us before daybreak, and send us to solitude with God. With this powerful reinforcement, prayer will conquer every opposing force and win victories from the jaws of hell.

We need men and women who will pray with power and with confidence that they can reach out, grapple God, and draw out His treasures for spiritual uses. Forceless prayers have no power to obtain answers, overcome difficulties, or gain complete and wonderful victories.

There are four things to remember when praying. God hears prayer, God considers prayer, God answers prayer, and God delivers by prayer. These things cannot be repeated too often. Prayer breaks all bars, dissolves all chains, opens all prisons, and widens all straits which bind God's saints.

Chapter 7

REFORMATION THROUGH PRAYER

"Before the Civil War there were many signs of a new interest in prayer and new hope from its exercise. These signs have multiplied. This one thing at least that is good the War has done for us already. Let us not miss our opportunity. Prayer is not an easy exercise. It requires encouragement, exposition, and training. There was never a time when men and women were more sincerely anxious to be told how to pray. Prayer is our mightiest weapon if we use it as God has encouraged us. We must do everything in our power to bring it into exercise"—Rev. James Hastings.

Ezra, a priest, and one of God's great reformers, is an Old Testament praying man who knew God's answer to prayer would overcome difficulties and bring good things to pass. He returned from Babylon under the patronage of the king of Babylon, who was strangely moved toward Ezra and who favored him in many ways.

Ezra had been in Jerusalem only a few days

when the princes came to him with the distressing information that Israel had not separated themselves from the people of Babylon and were practicing the abominations of the heathen nations surrounding them. What was worse was that the princes and rulers in Israel had been leaders in the trespass.

It was a sad state of affairs facing Ezra when he found Israel hopelessly involved with the world. God demands that His people, in all ages, keep themselves separated from the world. A separation so sharp that it can inspire antagonism. To this end, He put Israel in the Promised Land and cut them off from other nations by mountains, deserts, and seas. He immediately commanded them not to form any alliance with foreign nations, whether marital, social, or business.

In The Depths Of Sin

Ezra found Israel, as he returned from Babylon, paralyzed and thoroughly prostrated by the violation of this principle. They had intermarried, forming the closest and most sacred ties in family, social, and business life. Everyone was involved, priests, Levites, princes and the populace. The families, businesses, and religious lives of God's people were in violation of His law. What was to be done? What could be done? These were the important questions facing this leader of Israel, this man of God.

Everything appeared to be against Israel's recovery. Ezra could not preach to them, because the whole city would be inflamed, and the people would chase him out. What force was there which could recover them to God so that they would dissolve business partnerships, divorce wives and husbands, cut acquaintances, and dissolve friendships?

The first thing about Ezra which is worthy of remark was that he saw the situation and realized how serious it was. He was not a blind-eyed optimist who never saw anything wrong in Israel. By the mouth of Isaiah God had proposed the very pertinent question, "Who is blind but My servant?" (Isaiah 42:19).

But it could not possibly have applied to Ezra. Nor did he minimize the condition of things or seek to excuse the sins of the people or to minimize the enormity of their crimes. Their offense appeared in his eyes to be extremely serious. The leaders in Zion needed eyes to see the sins of Israel as well as the evils of the times. One great need of the modern Church is for leaders like Ezra who are not blind and who are willing to see the real state of the Church.

Naturally, seeing these dreadful evils in Israel and Jerusalem, he was distressed. The sad condition of things grieved him so much that he tore his garments, plucked his hair, and sat down in utter astonishment. All these things are evidences of his great distress at the terrible state of affairs. It was then, in that frame of mind, concerned, solicitous, and troubled in soul, that he gave himself to prayer, confessing the sins of the people and pleading for God's pardoning mercy. To whom should he go in a time like this but the God who hears prayer, who is ready to pardon, and who can bring the unexpected thing to pass?

Ezra was amazed beyond expression at the wicked conduct of the people. He was so deeply moved that he began to fast and pray. Prayer and fasting obtains results. He prayed with a broken heart, for there was nothing else he could do. He prayed to God, deeply burdened, prostrate on the ground and weeping, while the whole city united with him in prayer.

Prevailing Prayer

Prayer was the only way to appease God. Ezra became a great mover through prayer in a great work for God, with marvelous results. The whole work, its principles and its results, are summarized in Ezra 10:1: "Now when Ezra had prayed, and when he had confessed, weeping and casting himself down before the house of God, there assembled unto him out of Israel a very great congregation of men and women and children: for the people wept very sore."

There was mighty, simple, and persevering prayer. Intense and prevailing prayer had accomplished its end. Ezra's praying obtained results and brought a great work for God into being. It was mighty praying because it brought Almighty God to do His own work. Nothing but God and prayer could have changed this absolutely hopeless situation. But nothing is hopeless to prayer because nothing is hopeless to God.

Again we must say that prayer has only to do with God and only brings results if it has to do with God. Whatever influence the praying of Ezra had upon himself, prayer's chief—if not its only—result followed because it affected God and moved Him to do the work.

A great and general repentance followed Ezra's praying, and a wonderful reformation occurred in Israel. Ezra's mourning and praying were the great factors which brought these great things to pass.

So thorough was the revival that Scripture notes that Israel's leaders came to Ezra with these words:

"We have trespassed against our God, and have taken strange wives of the people of the land: Yet now there is hope in Israel concerning this thing.

"Now therefore let us make a covenant with our God to put away all the wives, and such as are born of them, according to the counsel of my lord, and of those that tremble at the commandment of our God; and let it be done according to the law.

"Arise, for this matter belongeth unto thee: we also will be with thee: be of good courage, and do it" (Ezra 10:2-4).

Chapter 8

PRAYER: THE BUILDER'S BLUEPRINT

"We do not care for your splendid abilities as a minister, or your natural endowment as an orator. We are sure that the truth of the matter is this: No one will or can command success and become a real praying soul unless intense application is the price. I am even now convinced that the difference between the saints like Wesley, Fletcher, Edwards, Brainerd, Bramwell, and ourselves is energy, perseverance, and invincible determination to succeed or die in the attempt. God help us"—Rev. Homer W. Hodge.

In telling of the praying saints of the Old Testament who obtained answers to prayer, we must not leave out Nehemiah, the builder. He stands on an equal footing with the others who have been considered. In the story of the reconstruction of Jerusalem after the Babylonian captivity, he played a prominent role. Prayer was also prominent in his life during those years. He was a captive in Babylon and had an important position in the palace of the king—he was the cup bearer. There must have been considerable merit in him to cause the king to take a Hebrew captive and place him in such an office. He had responsibility for the king's life, because he was in charge of the wine which the king drank.

Distress At Jerusalem's Captivity

One day while Nehemiah was in Babylon, in the king's palace, his brethren came from Jerusalem. Very naturally Nehemiah desired news about the people and information concerning the city itself. He heard the distressing news that the walls of Jerusalem were broken down, the gates were burned with fire, and those who were left at the beginning of the captivity were stigmatized and always in trouble.

Just one verse shows the effect of this sad news on this man of God:

"And it came to pass, when I heard these words, that I sat down and wept, and mourned certain days, and fasted, and prayed before the God of heaven" (Nehemiah 1:4).

Here was a man whose heart was in his native land, far away from where he lived. He loved Israel, was concerned for the welfare of Zion, and was true to God. Deeply distressed by the information concerning his brethren at Jerusalem, he mourned and wept. There are so few strong men today who can weep at the evils and abominations of the times! How rare are those who, seeing the desolations of God's people, are sufficiently interested and concerned for the welfare of the Church to mourn!

Mourning and weeping over the decay of religion, the decline of revival power, and the fearful inroads of worldliness in the Church are almost unknown. There is so much so-called optimism that leaders cannot see the breaking down of the walls of the Church and the low spiritual state of modern Christians. They have less heart to mourn and cry about it. Nehemiah was a mourner in Zion.

In this state of heart, distressed beyond measure, he did what other praying saints have done—he went to God and made the problem the subject of prayer. The prayer is recorded in the first chapter of Nehemiah and is a model for our prayers. He began with adoration, confessed the sins of his nation, pleaded the promises of God, mentioned former mercies, and begged for pardoning mercy.

Then he prayed with an eye to the future—for unquestionably the next time he was summoned into the king's presence he planned to ask permission to visit Jerusalem to try to remedy the distressing situation. He prayed for something very special: "And prosper, I pray Thee, Thy servant this day, and grant him mercy in the sight of this man. For," he adds by way of explanation, "I was the king's cup bearer" (Nehemiah 1:11).

It seemed all right to pray for his people. But how would a heathen king, with no sympathy whatever for the sad condition of Nehemiah's city and his people, consent to give up his faithful cup bearer allowing him to be gone for months? Nehemiah believed in a God who could respond and touch even the mind of a heathen ruler and move him favorably toward the request of his praying servant.

Nehemiah Goes To Jerusalem

When Nehemiah was summoned into the king's presence, God used the appearance of Nehemiah's countenance to gain the consent of Artaxerxes. This started the king's inquiry as to its cause, and the final result was that the king not only permitted Nehemiah to go back to Jerusalem, but furnished him with everything he needed for the journey and the success of the enterprise.

Nehemiah did not rest his case after he first prayed about this matter. He stated this significant fact as he talked to the king: "So I prayed unto the God of heaven" (Nehemiah 2:4). He gave the impression that while the king was inquiring about Nehemiah's request and the length of time he would be gone, he was then and there talking to God about the matter.

Nehemiah's intense, persistent praying prevailed. God can even affect the mind of a heathen ruler, and He can do this in answer to prayer without overturning the king's free choice or forcing his will. Esther's was a parallel case when she called upon her people to fast and pray for her as she went uninvited into the king's presence. As a result, at a very critical moment, his mind was touched by the Spirit of God, and he was favorably moved toward Esther holding out the golden scepter to her.

Rebuilding The Walls Of Jerusalem

Nor did Nehemiah's praying cease after he succeeded thus far. In building the wall of Jerusalem, he met great opposition from Sanballat and Tobiah, who ridiculed the efforts of the people to rebuild the city's walls. Unmoved by the derision and intense opposition of wicked opponents, he pursued his task. He mixed prayer with all he did: "Hear, O our God; for we are despised: and turn their reproach upon their own head, and give them for a prey in the land of our captivity" (Nehemiah 4:4). In continuing the account he says, "Nevertheless we made our prayer unto our God" (Nehemiah 4:9).

Prayer was prominent all through the accounts of the high and noble work Nehemiah was doing. God's replies were also prominent. Even after the walls were completed, these same enemies of God's people opposed Nehemiah again. But he renewed his praying, and he himself recorded this significant prayer: "Now therefore, O God, strengthen my hands" (Nehemiah 6:9).

Still further on, when Sanballat and Tobiah hired an emissary to frighten and hinder Nehemiah, he set himself directly against this new attack. Then again he turned to God in prayer: "My God, think Thou upon Tobiah and Sanballat according to these their works, and on the prophetess Noadiah, and the rest of the prophets, that would have put me in fear" (Nehemiah 6:14). God answered his faithful laborer and defeated the counsels and plans of Israel's wicked opponents.

Evil Practices In Israel

Nehemiah discovered, to his dismay, that the portions of the Levites had not been given them. As a result, the house of God was forsaken. He took steps to see that the lawful tithes were forthcoming so that God's house would be opened to all religious services. He even appointed treasurers to take charge of this business. Prayer must not be overlooked, so we find his prayer recorded at this time: "Remember me, O my God, concerning this, and wipe not out my good deeds that I have done for the house of my God, and for the offices thereof" (Nehemiah 13:14).

Do not think that this was a self-righteous plea like that of the Pharisee in our Lord's time. The Pharisee declared he was going up to the temple to pray and paraded his self-righteous claims in God's sight. It was a prayer like that of Hezekiah, who reminded God of his fidelity to Him and of his heart being right in His sight.

Once more Nehemiah found evil among the people of God. Just as he corrected the evil which caused the closing of God's house, he discovered Sabbath breaking. At this time he not only had to counsel the people and seek to correct them by mild means, but he also proposed to exercise his authority if they did not cease their buying and selling on the Sabbath day. He closed this part of his work with prayer, knowing God would hear him, and recorded his prayer on that occasion:

"Remember me, O my God, concerning this also, and spare me according to the greatness of Thy mercy" (Nehemiah 13:22).

Reform In Jerusalem

Lastly, as a reformer, he discovered another great evil among the people. They had intermarried with the men and women of Ashdod, Ammon, and Moab. Contending with them, he caused them to reform in this matter, and the close of his record has a prayer in it:

"Remember them, O my God, because they have defiled the priesthood, and the covenant of the priesthood, and of the Levites" (Nehemiah 13:29).

Cleansing them from all strangers, he appointed the wards of the priests and the Levites. His recorded career closes with this brief prayer: "Remember me, O my God, for good" (Nehemiah 13:31).

Blessed is the Church whose leaders are men of prayer. Happy is that congregation which contemplates the building of a church so that it will include leaders who will lay its foundations in prayer and whose walls go up side by side with prayer. Through prayer God builds churches and erects the walls of houses of worship. Through prayer God defeats the opponents of those who are prosecuting His enterprises. Prayer favorably touches minds, even those not connected with the Church, and moves them in favor of Church matters. Prayer helps mightily in all matters concerning God's cause. It wonderfully aids and encourages the hearts of those who have His work in hand in this world.

Chapter 9

RAISE YOUR CHILDREN FOR GOD

"It was a grand action by Jerome, one of the Roman fathers. He laid aside all pressing engagements and went to fulfill the call God gave him, which was to translate the Holy Scriptures. His congregations were larger than many preachers' of today; but he said to his people, 'Now it is necessary that the Scriptures be translated, you must find another minister. I am bound for the wilderness and shall not return until my task is finished.' Away he went and labored and prayed until he produced the Latin Vulgate which will last as long as the world stands. So we must say to our friends, 'I must go away and take time for prayer and solitude.' And though we do not write Latin Vulgates, our work will be immortal: Glory to God"—Rev. C.H. Spurgeon.

Samuel was born in direct answer to prayer. His praying mother's heart was full of earnest desire for a son. He came into life under prayer surroundings, and his first months in this world were spent in direct contact with a woman who knew how to pray. It was a prayer accompanied by the solemn vow that if he was given to her, he would be "lent to the Lord" (1 Samuel 1:28).

True to that vow, this praying mother put him directly in touch with the minister of the sanctuary and under the influence of the house of prayer. It was no wonder he developed into a man of prayer. We could not have expected otherwise with such a beginning in life and with such early environments. Such surroundings always make impressions upon children and tend to mold character and determine destiny.

Raised In Righteousness

He was in a favorable place to hear God when He spoke to him, and he was in an atmosphere which nurtured his heeding the divine call that came to him. It was the most natural thing in the world when, at the third call from heaven, he recognized God's voice. His childish heart responded promptly, "Speak; for Thy servant heareth" (1 Samuel 3:10). There was a quick response from his boyish spirit, of submission, willingness, and prayer.

If he had been born to a different sort of mother, if he had been placed in different surroundings, if he had spent his early days in contact with different influences, he may not have heard God's voice and so readily yielded his young life to God. Would a worldly home, with worldly surroundings, with a worldly-minded mother, separated from the will of God, have produced such a character as Samuel? It takes godly influences in early life to produce such praying men as Samuel.

Would you have your child called early into divine service and separated from the world to God? Would you have him situated so that he could be called in childhood by the Spirit of God? Put him under prayer influences. Place him near and directly under the influence of a man or woman of God and in close touch with the house of prayer. God will honor your action.

Samuel knew God in boyhood. As a consequence, he knew God in manhood. He recognized God in childhood, obeyed Him, and prayed to Him. The result was that he recognized God in manhood, obeyed Him, and prayed to Him. If more children were born of praying parents, brought up in direct contact with the house of prayer, and reared in prayer environments, more children would hear the voice of God's Spirit speaking to them. They would respond quicker to those divine calls to a religious life.

Do we want to have praying men in our churches? We must have praying mothers to give them birth, praying homes to influence their lives, and praying surroundings to impress their minds and to lay the foundations for praying lives. Praying Samuels come from praying Hannahs. Praying priests come from the house of prayer. Praying leaders come from praying homes.

Prayer Brings Repentance

For years Israel was under bondage to the Philistines. The ark was housed in the home of Abinadab whose son, Eleazer, was appointed to keep this sacred testimony of God. The people had turned to idolatry, and Samuel was disturbed about the religious condition of the nation. The ark of God was absent, the people enjoyed worshipping idols, and there was a grievous departure from God.

Calling upon them to put away their strange gods, Samuel urged them to prepare their hearts for the Lord and begin to serve Him again. He promised them that the Lord would deliver them out of the hands of the Philistines. Samuel was a preacher of the times. He made a deep impression and bore rich fruits, as such preaching always does. "Then the children of Israel did put away Baalim and Ashtaroth, and served the Lord only" (1 Samuel 7:4).

But this was not enough. Prayer had to accompany their reformation. So Samuel, true to his convictions about prayer, said to the people, "Gather all Israel to Mizpeh, and I will pray for you unto the Lord" (1 Samuel 7:5). While Samuel was offering up prayer for these wicked Israelites, the Philistines were preparing for battle against the nation. But, in answer to prayer, the Lord intervened at the critical moment with a great thunderstorm, defeated the enemy, "and they were smitten before Israel" (1 Samuel 7:10).

Fortunately the nation had a man who could pray and who knew the worth of prayer. He was a leader who had God's ear and who could influence God.

But Samuel's praying did not stop there. He judged Israel all the days of his life. Every year he made a circuit through Bethel, Gilgal, and Mizpeh. Then he returned home to Ramah. "And there he built an altar unto the Lord" (1 Samuel 7:17). It was an altar of sacrifice, but it was also an altar of prayer.

While the altar may have been for the benefit of his community, it must have also been a family altar. At the altar, Almighty God was acknowledged in the home. The altar was the advertisement of a religious home. Here father and mother would call upon the Lord. The altar differentiated this home from all the worldly and idolatrous homes surrounding them. Blessed is that home where daily thanksgiving ascends to heaven and where praying is done at the altar morning and night.

Samuel was not only a praying priest, a praying leader, and a praying teacher, but he was also a praying father. The great need of these modern times is for Christian homes to have praying mothers and fathers. This is where the breakdown in religion occurs, where the religious life of a community first begins to decay, and where we must go first to raise praying men and women in God's Church. The revival must start in the home.

A King Instead Of God

A crisis came to this nation. The people were

infatuated by the glory of a kingdom with a human king, and they were prepared to reject God as their King. God had always been their King. They came to Samuel with the bold request, "Make us a king to judge us like all the nations" (1 Samuel 8:5).

The idea displeased this man of God, who was jealous for the name, the honor, and the pleasure of the Lord God. How could it be otherwise? Who would not have been displeased if he thought like Samuel? It grieved his soul. The Lord, however, came to him with the comforting assurance, "Hearken unto the voice of the people, in all that they say unto thee they have not rejected thee, but they have rejected Me, that I should not reign over them" (1 Samuel 8:7).

It was then that Samuel followed the bent of his mind, "and Samuel prayed unto the Lord" (1 Samuel 8:6). It seemed that in every matter concerning this people, Samuel had to pray over it. The need was greater when the people wanted an entire revolution in the form of government, replacing God with a human king. Samuel wanted to know what God thought about this. Praying men are needed to carry the affairs of government to God in prayer. Lawmakers, judges, and lawyers need leaders, who know God, to pray for them. There would be fewer mistakes if there was more praying done in civil matters.

But this was not to be the end of this matter. God had to show definitely and plainly His displeasure at such a request, that the people would know what a wicked thing they had done, even though God consented to their request. They had to know God still existed and was active in the lives of His people, their king, and the affairs of government.

So the prayers of Samuel were again brought into play to carry out the divine purposes. Samuel told the people to stand still, so he could show them what the Lord would do. He called upon God, and in answer God sent a tremendous thunderstorm which terrified the people and caused them to acknowledge their great sin.

The people were so afraid that they hastily called upon Samuel to pray for them and to spare them from what seemed to be destruction. Samuel prayed again; God heard and answered; and the thunder and rain ceased.

A Sinful King

One more incident in the prayer life of Samuel is worth noticing. King Saul was ordered to destroy all the Amalekites, root and branch, and all of their goods. But Saul, contrary to divine instructions, spared King Agag and the best of the sheep and the cattle. He justified it by claiming that the people wanted it done.

God then brought this message to Samuel:

"It repenteth Me that I have set up Saul to be king: for he is turned back from following Me, and hath not performed My commandments" (1 Samuel 15:11).

"And it grieved Samuel; and he cried unto the

Lord all night" (1 Samuel 15:11). Such a sudden declaration was enough to produce grief in the soul of a man like Samuel, who loved his nation, who was true to God, and who above everything else desired the prosperity of Zion. Today such grief over the evils of the Church should still drive a man to his knees in prayer.

Of course, Samuel carried the problem to God. It was a time for prayer. The circumstance was too serious for him not to be deeply moved to pray. The inner soul of Samuel was so greatly disturbed that he prayed all night about it. Too much was at stake for him to shut his eyes to the affair, to treat it indifferently, and to let it pass without taking God into the matter. The future welfare of Israel was in the balance. Samuel's childhood was greatly influenced by prayer. When he became a leader over Israel, he obtained answers to prayer because of his long time communion with the Lord.

Chapter 10

PRAYING IN CAPTIVITY

"It is a wonderful historical fact that men of prayer have always been men of power in the world. If you are debating with some friend in the workshop, be sure and ask him why it is that the men of power in the world have always been the men of prayer"—Bishop Winnington Ingram.

Daniel took a chance when he refused to obey the Babylonian king who ordered him not to petition God or king for thirty days. The penalty was to be thrown into the lion's den. However, Daniel paid no attention to the edict, for it is recorded, "Now when Daniel knew that the writing was signed, he went into his house; and his windows being open in his chamber toward Jerusalem, he kneeled upon his knees three times a day, and prayed, and gave thanks before his God, as he did aforetime" (Daniel 6:10).

Do not forget that this was Daniel's regular habit. "He kneeled upon his knees and prayed as he did aforetime." What was the result? He was thrown to the lions just as expected. God responded by sending an angel into the den of lions with Daniel and locked their mouths so that not a hair on his head was touched, and he was wonderfully delivered. Even so today, deliverance always comes to God's saints who tread the path of prayer as the saints of old.

Faithful Despite Circumstances

Even though Daniel was away from the house of God and deprived of religious privileges, he did not forget God while he was in a foreign land. He is a striking illustration of a young man who was decidedly religious under the most unfavorable circumstances. He proved conclusively that one could definitely be a servant of God though his environment was anything but religious. He was among heathens as far as a God-fearing nation was concerned. There was no temple worship, no Sabbath day, no Word of God to be read. But he had one help which remained with him, and of which he could not be deprived. That was his secret prayers, and his assurance that God would answer him.

The King's Mysterious Dream

Resolving in his heart, without debating the question, not to eat the king's meat or drink the king's wine, he stood out in that ungodly country as a striking illustration of a young man who feared God. He was determined to be religious, no matter what the cost. But he did not have a flowery bed on which to rest or a smooth road on which to travel.

The whimsical, tyranical, and unreasonable king, Nebuchadnezzar, put him to the test and proved his praying qualities. This king had a strange dream, the details of which he forgot, but the fact of the dream remained. He was so troubled about the dream that he called for all the soothsayers, astrologers, and sorcerers to recall the dream and then interpret it.

He classed Daniel and his three companions, Shadrach, Meshach, and Abednego, with these men, though there really was nothing they had in common with the others. Daniel and his men knew that it was impossible to discover a dream like that. They then asked the king to tell the dream to them, saying they would interpret it. The king became very angry, and he ordered them to be put to death.

But Daniel leaped into action. At his suggestion, the execution of the rash edict was held up. He immediately called his three companions into counsel. Urging them to unite with him in prayer, Daniel asked God to show him the dream as well as the interpretation. In answer to this united praying, it is recorded: "Then was the secret revealed unto Daniel in a night vision. Then Daniel blessed the God of heaven" (Daniel 2:19).

As a sequel to the praying session of these four men, Daniel revealed to the king his dream and its interpretation. As a result, the king acknowledged God and elevated Daniel and his three associates to high positions. It all came about because there was a praying man available at a critical time.

Blessed is that nation which has praying men who can aid civil rulers who are greatly perplexed and in great difficulty. Blessed is a nation composed of praying men who can be depended upon to pray for rulers of state and Church.

Angels Bring Answers

Years afterward, while still in a foreign land, Daniel still had not forgotten the God of his fathers. He was given the noted vision of the "Ram and the He Goat." Daniel, however, did not comprehend this strange vision, yet he knew it was from God and had a deep and future meaning for nations and people. So he followed the bent of his religious mind and prayed about it.

"And it came to pass, when I, even I Daniel, had seen the vision, and sought for the meaning, then, behold, there stood before me as the appearance of a man.

"And I heard a man's voice, which called, and said, Gabriel, make this man to understand the vision" (Daniel 9:15-16).

And so Gabriel made him understand the full meaning of this remarkable vision. But understanding only came in answer to Daniel's praying. Puzzling questions may often find the answer in prayer. And, as elsewhere, God employed angelic means to convey information and prayer answers. Angels are very involved with prayer. Praying men and the angels of heaven are in close touch with each other.

Some years thereafter, Daniel was studying the records of the nation, and he discovered that it was about time for the seventy years of captivity of his people to end. So he prayed:

"And I set my face unto the Lord God, to seek by prayer and supplications, with fasting, and sackcloth, and ashes: And I prayed unto the Lord my God, and made my confession" (Daniel 9:3-4).

Then follows the record in Old Testament Scripture of Daniel's prayer. It was full of meaning, so simple in its delivery, so earnest in its spirit, and so direct in its confession and requests. It is worthy of being an example for our prayers.

It was while he was speaking in prayer that the same archangel, Gabriel, who seemed to have a direct interest in this man's praying "being caused to fly swiftly, touched me about the time of the evening oblation. And he informed me, and talked with me" (Daniel 9:21-22). And then Gabriel gave Daniel the valuable information.

The angels of God are much nearer to us in our intervals of prayer than we imagine. God employs these glorious, heavenly beings in the blessed work of hearing and answering prayer. Usually the prayer, as in the case of Daniel on this occasion, deals with the present and future welfare of His people.

Cause Of Delayed Answers

One other praying incident in the life of this captive man in Babylon is noteworthy. Daniel had another revelation, but the time of its fulfillment appeared to be far in the future. "In those days I Daniel was mourning three full weeks. I ate no pleasant bread, neither came flesh nor wine into my mouth, till three whole weeks were fulfilled" (Daniel 10:2-3).

It was then that he had a very strange experience and that a strange angelic being gave him a still stranger revelation. It is worthwhile to read the Scripture account:

"And, behold, an hand touched me, which set me upon my knees and upon the palms of my hands.

"And he said unto me, O Daniel, a man greatly beloved, understand the words that I speak unto thee, and stand upright: for unto thee am I now sent. And when he had spoken this word unto me, I stood trembling.

"Then said he unto me, Fear not, Daniel: for from the first day that thou didst set thine heart to understand, and to chasten thyself before thy God thy words were heard, and I am come for thy words.

"But the Prince of the kingdom of Persia withstood me one and twenty days: but, lo, Michael, one of the chief princes, came to help me and I remained there with the kings of Persia" (Daniel 10:10-13).

What all this means is difficult to comprehend, but enough appears on its face to lead us to believe that the angels in heaven are deeply interested in our praying and are sent to tell us the answers to our prayers. Further, it is very clear that some unseen forces or invisible spirits are operating to hinder the answers to our prayers. Exactly who the prince of Persia was who withstood this great angelic being is not divulged. But enough is revealed to know that there must be a contest in the unseen world about us between spirits sent to minister to us in answer to our prayers and the devil and his evil spirits who seek to defeat these good spirits.

The passage furthermore gives us some hint as to why we do not obtain answers to prayer immediately. For "three full weeks" Daniel mourned and prayed, and for "one and twenty days" the divinely appointed angel was opposed by the "Prince of the kingdom of Persia."

Daniel was wise to continue praying, maintaining his courage, fortitude, and determination, and persisting in his praying for three weeks while the fearful conflict between good and bad spirits raged about him, unseen by mortal eyes. It would be well for us if we do not give up in our praying when God seems not to hear and the answer is not immediate. It takes time to pray, and it takes time to get the answer.

Delays in answering prayer are not denials.

Failure to receive an immediate answer is not evidence that God does not hear prayer. It takes not only courage and persistence to pray successfully, but a lot of patience as well. "Wait on the Lord: be of good courage, and He shall strengthen thine heart: wait, I say, on the Lord" (Psalm 27:14).

Chapter 11

FAITH OF SINNERS IN PRAYER

"A certain preacher, whose sermons converted many souls, received a revelation from God. It said it was not his sermons or works, but the prayers of an illiterate lay brother who sat on the pulpit steps pleading for the success of the sermon. It was this brother's prayers which brought men to the Lord. This could be the case with us as well. It may be that after laboring long and wearily, without good prayer, all honor belongs to another builder whose prayers were gold, silver, and precious stones; while our sermonizing, being apart from prayer, are but hay and stubble"—Rev. C.H. Spurgeon.

One of the peculiar features of prayer, as we study the Old Testament on this subject, is the faith of unrighteous and backslidden men in prayer. They had great confidence that God would answer the prayers of praying men of that day. The backslidden knew certain men were men of prayer who believed in God, who were favored by God, and who prayed to God. They recognized these men as having influence with God in averting wrath and in giving deliverance from evil.

Frequently, when in trouble, when God's wrath was threatened, and even when evil fell upon them for their iniquities, the unrighteous showed their faith in prayer by appealing to the men who prayed. These sinners wanted God's favored ones to beg God to avert His displeasure and turn aside His wrath against them. Recognizing the value of prayer as a divine agency to save men, they implored the men who prayed to intercede with God for them. They knew God answered a righteousness man's prayers.

One of the strange paradoxes of those early days is that while people departed from God, going into grievous sin, they did not become atheists or unbelievers in the existence of a prayer-answering God. Wicked men held fast to a belief in God's existence and to faith in the power of prayer to secure pardon for sin and to deliver them from His wrath.

It is worthy to note the influence of Christianity on sinners who believe in a Christian's prayer for them. It is an item of interest and an important event when a sinner on a dying bed calls for a praying man to come to his bedside to pray for him. It is meaningful when penitent sinners, under a sense of their guilt, feel the displeasure of God, approach a church altar, and say, "Pray for me, you praying men and women."

Little does the Church understand its full impact nor appreciate the full significance of prayer. This is especially true for the unsaved men and women who ask for prayer for their immortal souls. If the Church was fully attuned to God's willingness to respond, awake to the real peril of the unconverted all about it, more sinners would seek the altars of the Church crying out to praying people, "Pray for my soul!"

There may be much so-called praying for sinners, but it is cold, formal, official praying which never reaches God and accomplishes nothing. Revivals begin when sinners seek the prayers of praying people and then begin to seek the God who answers those prayers.

Faith Of Wicked Men In Prayer

Several things stand out in bold relief as we look at those Old Testament days.

First there was the tendency of sinners against God to almost involuntarily turn to praying men for help and refuge when trouble drew near. They requested prayers for relief and deliverance. "Pray for us!" was their cry.

Second there was the readiness with which those praying men responded to these appeals and prayed to God for those who desired deliverance. Moreover, it is impressive that these praying men were always in the spirit of prayer and ready at any time to seek God's reply. They were always excited about prayer.

Third, we note the wonderful influence these men of prayer had with God when they made their appeal to Him. God nearly always responded quickly and heard their praying for others. Intercessory prayer predominated in those early days of the Church.

How far the present-day Church is responsible for the unbelief of today's sinners in the value of prayer is a question worthy of earnest consideration.

The first illustration we notice showing the faith of wicked men in prayer, and their appeal for a man of God to intercede for them, is when the fiery serpents were sent upon the Israelites. They were journeying from Mount Hor by way of the Red Sea, seeking to circle the land of Edom, when they spoke against God and Moses:

"Wherefore have ye brought us up out of Egypt to die in the wilderness? for there is no bread, neither is there any water; and our soul loatheth this light bread" (Numbers 21:5).

This complaining so displeased God that He sent fiery serpents among the people causing many of the Israelites to die.

"Therefore the people came to Moses, and said, We have sinned for we have spoken against the Lord, and against thee; pray unto the Lord, that He take away the serpents from us" (Numbers 21:7).

And Moses prayed for the people. God answered his prayer.

As far as these people had departed from God, and as great as was their sin in complaining against God's dealings with them, they had not lost faith in obtaining answers to prayer. Neither did they forget that there was a leader in Israel who had influence with God in prayer; nor did they forget that he could—by prayer—avert disaster and bring deliverance to them.

Guilty Ruler Pleads For Intercession

Jeroboam, first king of the ten tribes when the kingdom was divided, is another case in point. This case is famous because of the notoriety of his departure from God, which was often referred to in the later history of Israel as "the sins of Jeroboam the son of Nebat" (2 Kings 10:29). His life shows that, despite his great wickedness, he did not lose his faith in the powerful effectiveness of prayer. He knew God acted as a result of prayer. This king presumed to take the place of the high priest and stood by the altar to burn incense.

A man of God came out of Judah and cried against the altar and proclaimed, "Behold the altar shall be rent, and the ashes that are upon it shall be poured out" (1 Kings 13:3). This angered Jeroboam, who saw that it was intended as a public rebuke for him because it was contrary to the Levitical law to assume the office of God's priest. The king even put forth his hand with the apparent purpose of arresting or doing violence to the man of God and said, "Lay hold on him" (1 Kings 13:4).

Immediately God smote the king with leprosy so that he could not pull his hand back again. At the same time, the altar was rent. Astonished and afraid beyond measure at this lightning retribution for his sin, Jeroboam cried out to the man of God,

"Intreat now the face of the Lord thy God, and pray for me, that my hand may be restored me again" (1 Kings 13:6). And it is recorded that "the man of God besought the Lord, and the king's hand was restored him again, and became as it was before" (1 Kings 13:6).

Let us keep in mind that we are not now considering the praying habits of the man of God or the possibilities of prayer, though both face us here. But rather, we find here that a ruler in Israel, who is guilty of a serious sin, immediately calls upon a praying man to intercede with God in his behalf when God's wrath falls upon him. It is another case where a sinner showed his faith that God would answer the prayers of a holy man. Sad is the day in a Christian land when there is decay of prayer in the Church and when sinners are so unaffected by the religion of the Church that they have no faith in prayer and care little about the prayers of praying men.

King Jeroboam illustrated his faith in prayer again when his son fell sick and was about to die. This wicked, indifferent king sent his wife off to Ahijah, the prophet of God, to ask him to give the outcome of the child's illness. She attempted to deceive the old prophet, who was nearly blind, intending not to make herself known to him. But he had the vision of a prophet, even though nearly blind, and immediately revealed that he recognized her.

After telling her many important things concerning the kingdom and charging that her husband had not kept God's commandments, but had gone into idolatry, he said to her, "Arise, thou therefore, get thee down to thine own house: and when thy feet enter into the city, the child shall die" (1 Kings 14:12).

How natural it is for a father in trouble to appeal to a praying prophet for relief! As in the first case, his sin did not blind his eyes to the value of having a man of God intercede for him. Jeroboam knew God would respond. It accomplished nothing, but it did prove our contention that in Old Testament times sinners, while they were not themselves praying men, believed strongly in the prayers of praying men.

Praying Men Obtain Answers

Take for instance, Johanan who lived just as the children of Israel began their life of captivity in Babylon. Johanan and Jeremiah, with a small company, were left in their native land. Ishmael conspired against Gedaliah, the appointed governor of the country, and had slain him. Johanan came to the rescue delivering the people from Ishmael who was taking them away from their land. But Johanan wanted to flee down into Egypt, contrary to the divine plan. At this point he assembled all the people, and they went to Jeremiah with the earnest appeal:

"We beseech thee, let our supplication be accepted before thee, and pray for us unto the Lord thy God. . .that the Lord thy God may shew us the way wherein we may walk, and the thing that we may do" (Jeremiah 42:2-3).

Like all other appeals to good men for prayer, Jeremiah interceded for these seekers of the right way. After ten days the answer came. Jeremiah informed them that God said they should not go down to Egypt, but remain in and about Jerusalem. But Johanan and the people refused to do as God told them. Their disobedience, however, does not disprove the fact that they had faith in prayer and in praying men.

Another case may be noticed as showing the truth of our proposition that Old Testament sinners had faith in prayer, thus indirectly proving the preeminence of prayer in those days. These sinners believed prayer brought results. Certainly prayer must have had a prominent place, and its necessity must have been generally recognized, when even sinners, by their actions, endorsed its virtue and necessity.

Surely, if sinners bore testimony to its worth, modern Church people ought to have a deep sense of its need and should have strong faith in prayer and its virtue. If the men of Old Testament times had a reputation as praying men, then in this favored day, Christian men should prize prayer so that they would also have a wide reputation as praying men.

Zedekiah was king of Judah just as the captivity of God's people began. He was in charge of the kingdom when Jerusalem was besieged by the king of Babylon. It was just about this time that Zedekiah sent two chosen men to Jeremiah saying:

"Inquire, I pray thee, of the Lord for us; for Nebuchadrezzar king of Babylon maketh war against us; if so be that the Lord will deal with us according to all His wondrous works, that he may go up and from us" (Jeremiah 21:2).

And God told Jeremiah, in answer to this inquiry, what to do and what would occur. But as in the case of Johanan, Zedekiah proved unfaithful and would not do as God instructed. This turning to prayer proved conclusively that Zedekiah had not lost his faith in prayer as a means of finding out the mind of God, nor did it affect him in his belief in the virtue of the prayers of a praying man.

Truly, prayer had a preeminent place in all Old Testament history when not only the men of God were noted for obtaining answers to prayer, but even disloyal, sinful men testified to the virtue of prayer.

Chapter 12

LESSONS IN PRAYER

"Fletcher of Madeley, a great teacher of the 18th century used to lecture young theological students. He was a fellow worker with Wesley, and a man of most saintly character. When he lectured on one of the great topics of the Word of God, such as the fullness of God's Holy Spirit or on the power and blessing that He meant His people to have, he would close the lecture and say, 'That is the theory. Now will those who want the practice come along up to my room?' Again and again they closed their books and went away to his room where the hour's theory would be followed by one or two hours of prayer"— Rev. Hubert Brooke.

Paul felt the urgent need for prayer so much that his encouragement to Christians to pray was often strenuous, pleading, and persistent. "I exhort," he wrote to Timothy, "that first of all, supplications, prayers, intercessions, and giving of thanks, be made for all men" (1 Timothy 2:1). Prayer was to be the greatest security and truth for the Church.

First and foremost, the Church of Christ was to be a praying Church. It was to pray for all men.

Paul instructed the Philippians this way: "Be careful for nothing; but in every thing by prayer and supplication with thanksgiving let your requests be made known unto God" (Philippians 4:6). The Church is to be anxious about nothing. Every need and request must be made through prayer. Nothing is too small for prayer. Nothing is too great for God to overcome. God will answer and take care of the Church's needs.

Paul wrote a vital command to the church at Thessalonica, "Rejoice evermore. Pray without ceasing. In everything give thanks: for this is the will of God in Christ Jesus concerning you" (1 Thessalonians 5:16-18). The Church, in order to obtain answers, must devote itself to unceasing prayer. Never was prayer to cease in the Church. This is God's will concerning His Church on earth.

Direction Through Prayer

Paul was not only devoted to prayer himself, but he continually and earnestly urged it in a way that showed its vital importance. He not only insisted that the Church pray, but he urged persistent praying. "Continue in prayer, and watch in the same" (Colossians 4:2) was the keynote of all his exhortations on prayer. "Praying always with all prayer and supplication" (Ephesians 6:18) was the way he pressed this important matter upon the people. He exhorted, "that men pray everywhere, lifting up holy hands, without wrath and doubting" (1

Timothy 2:8). Because he prayed this way himself, he could justify encouraging those to whom he ministered.

Paul was an appointed leader and a leader by universal recognition and acceptance. He had many mighty miracles occur in his ministry. His conversion, so conspicuous and radical, was a great miracle. His call to the apostleship was clear, luminous, and convincing. But these were not the most divine manifestations of God which brought forth the largest results in his ministry. Paul's course was more distinctly shaped and his career rendered more powerfully successful because of his prayer communication with God. He knew God would answer his prayers with guidance and provision.

It is no surprise then that he gave so much prominence to prayer in his preaching and writing. Because prayer was the highest exercise in his personal life, prayer assumed the same high place in his teaching. His personal example of prayer and its answers added force to his teaching. His practice and his teaching ran on parallel lines. There was no inconsistency between the two parts of his life.

Paul was the chief of the apostles and the chief in prayer. He was the foremost of the apostles because of his prayer life. Therefore, he was qualified to be a teacher on prayer. His praying fitted him to teach others what prayer was and what prayer could do. For this reason he was capable of urging the people to not neglect prayer since so much depended upon it.

He who wants to teach others to receive answers to prayer must first himself be devoted to prayer. He who urges prayer on others must first tread the path of prayer himself. Preachers will encourage the practice of praying in proportion to the quality of their prayer life. The quality of their sermons will also depend on the quality of their prayer life. Since that course of reasoning is true, it would be legitimate to draw the conclusion that the reason there is so little preaching on how to receive answers to prayer today is because preachers themselves do not know how.

We might stake the whole question of the absolute necessity and the possibilities of prayer in this dispensation on Paul's attitude toward prayer. If personal force, if the energy of a strong will, if profound convictions, if personal culture and talents, if any one of these, or all of them united, could direct the Church of God without prayer, then logically prayer would be unnecessary.

If profound piety and unswerving consecration to a high purpose, if impassioned loyalty to Jesus Christ, if any or all of these could exist without devoted prayer, or lift a Church leader above the necessity of prayer, then Paul was above its use. But prayer brings God's response and direction. Even Paul, the great, gifted, favored, and devoted apostle, felt the necessity of unceasing prayer. He realized that its practice was urgent and pressing, that the Church should pray without ceasing. Today, also, the brethren in the apostolate should be aided by universal and mighty praying.

Paul's praying, his commands, and the urgency with which he encouraged the Church to pray, is the most convincing proof of the absolute necessity of prayer. Prayer is a great moral force in the world, an indispensable and inalienable factor in the progress and spread of the gospel. Prayer was the means of communicating with God, asking His direction. It is also key in the development of personal piety. In Paul's view, no Church could succeed without answered prayer.

To pray *everywhere,* to pray *in everything,* and to pray *without ceasing,* was Paul's reply to the question regarding unanswered prayer.

Holy Spirit's Prayer Doctrine

Timothy was very dear to Paul, and the attachment was mutual and intensified by all their similar characteristics. Paul found in Timothy those elements which enabled him to be his spiritual successor. Paul was the leader of the great spiritual principles which were essential to the establishment and prosperity of the Church. These primary and vital truths he drilled into Timothy. Paul regarded Timothy as one to whom fundamental and vital truths might be committed, who would preserve them truly, and who would commit them, without corruption, to the future. So he gave Timothy this deposit of prayer for all ages.

Before we go any further, note that Paul wrote directly under the supervision of the Holy Spirit, who guarded Paul against error and who suggested the truths which Paul taught. We believe, without compromise in the least, in the absolute inspiration of the Scriptures, and Paul's writings are part of those Sacred Writings. This being true, the doctrine of prayer which Paul affirmed is the doctrine of the Holy Spirit. His epistles are of the Word of God, inspired, authentic, and of divine authority. So that prayer as taught by Paul is the doctrine which Almighty God would have His Church accept, believe, and practice. God does not want His Church to be without His provision and direction as given through prayer.

These words to Timothy, therefore, were divinely inspired words. This section of Scripture is much more than suggestive and is far more than a broad, bare outline on prayer. It instructs about prayer, about how men ought to pray, how businessmen should pray, and the reasons why men ought to pray, and it needs to be strongly and insistently emphasized.

Elements Of Prayer

Here are Paul's words to Timothy on prayer:

"I exhort therefore, that, first of all, supplications, prayers, intercessions, and giving of thanks, be made for all men;

"For kings, and for all that are in authority; that we may lead a quiet and peaceable life in all godliness and honesty.

"For this is good and acceptable in the sight of God our Saviour;

"Who will have all men to be saved, and to

come unto the knowledge of the truth.

"For there is one God, and one mediator between God and men, the man Christ Jesus;

"Who gave Himself a ransom for all, to be testified in due time. I will therefore that men pray everywhere, lifting up holy hands, without wrath and doubting" (1 Timothy 2:1-6,8).

In this prayer section, Paul has illustrated the inheritance and practice of every Christian in all ages. It gives us a view of the energetic and multifaceted characteristics of prayer. Prayer comes first. It must be first in all occupations. So exacting and imperative in its significance and power is prayer that it stands first among spiritual values. He that prays not, is not at all. He is nothing, less than nothing. He is below zero, so far as Jesus Christ and God are concerned. How can a man's needs be met or those of the Church or those of the country, if he does not ask of the Lord?

Paul's teaching is that praying is the most important of all activities on earth. Everything else must be restrained, retired, to give it primacy. Put it first, and keep it first. Defeat, not victory, lies in making prayer secondary. Making prayer subordinate is to fetter and destroy its power. If God and prayer are put first, then victory is assured. Prayer must either reign in life or must abdicate. Which shall it be?

Affected By Prayer

According to Paul, "supplications, prayers, intercessions and giving of thanks" all these elements and forms of prayer are to be offered in intercession for men. Prayer is offered for things, for all temporal good, and for all spiritual good and grace. But in these directions Paul rises to the highest results and purposes of prayer. Men are to be affected by prayer. Their benefit, character, conduct, and destiny are all involved in answered prayer.

In this regard, prayer moves along the highest plane and pursues its loftiest goal. Since we live in the world, we must be concerned with material things like our possessions and jobs. However, our main purpose in this life is to pray for other men. This broadens and ennobles prayer. Men, despite the range of their spiritual conditions, are to be held in the mighty grasp of prayer.

Without Wrath

Paul's teaching states that prayer is essentially a thing of the inner nature. The Spirit within us prays. Note Paul's directions: "I will therefore that men pray everywhere, without wrath" (1 Timothy 2:8). "Wrath" is a term which denotes the natural, internal motion of plants and fruits, swelling with juice. The natural juices are warmed into life and rise by the warmth of spring.

Man has in him natural juices which rise also. Warmth, heat, all stages of passions and desires, every degree of feeling, these spontaneously rise under provocation. Guard against and supress them. Man cannot pray with these natural feelings rising in him, cultivated, cherished, and continued within.

Prayer is to be without these. "Without wrath." Higher, better, nobler inspirations are to lift prayer upward. "Wrath" depresses prayer, hinders it, suppresses it. The word "without" means making no use of, having no association with, apart from, aloof from. The natural, unrenewed heart has no part in praying. Its heat and all of its natural juices poison and destroy praying. The essence of prayer is deeper than nature. We cannot pray by nature, not even the kindliest and the best nature.

During Distress

Prayer is the true test of character. Fidelity to our conditions and trueness to our relatives are often indicated by our prayerfulness. These qualities come as answers to prayer. Some conditions give birth to prayer. They are the soil which germinates and perfects prayer. To pray under some circumstances seems very fitting. Not to pray in some conditions seems heartless and discordant. The natural and providential conditions of prayer are the great storms of life—when we are helpless and without relief or are devoid of comfort, God is most willing to aid and comfort us.

Widowhood is a great sorrow. It comes to saintly women as well as to others. Widows are to be honored especially since their sorrow is deep. Their piety is aromatic and lightened by their bruised hearts. Here is Paul's description of such widows:

"Now she that is a widow indeed, and desolate,

trusteth in God, and continueth in supplications and prayers night and day. But she that liveth in pleasure is dead while she liveth" (1 Timothy 5:5-6).

Here is the striking contrast between two types of women. One devoted her time to supplication and prayer night and day. The other lived in sinful pleasure and was spiritually dead. Paul describes a faithful widow as being great in prayer. Her prayers, born of her faith and desolation, are a mighty force. Day and night her prayers go up to God—unceasingly. The widowed heart receives help from God when that heart is found in the way of prayer, intense, unwearied prayer.

One of Paul's striking directions, worthy of study, is this, "continuing instant in prayer" (Romans 12:12), or, as the Revised Standard Version reads, "Be constant in prayer" (Romans 12:12). This is Paul's description of prayer. The term means to remain, to be steadfast and faithful without hesitating, to stick to it, to continue with strength to the end.

An Occupation

Praying is an occupation, a life-long business to be followed with diligence, fervor, and toil. The Christian's foremost purpose is prayer. It is his most engaging, most heavenly, most lucrative business. Prayer is a commission of such high dignity and importance that it is to be performed without ceasing. In other words without let up or break down, followed assiduously and without intermission. Prayer must cover all things, be in every place, find itself in all seasons, and embrace everything, always, and everywhere.

In the remarkable prayer in the third chapter of Ephesians, Paul is praying for wide reaches of religious experience. He is bowing his knees before God, in the name of Jesus Christ, asking God to grant that these Ephesian believers would experience the fullness of Jesus' love, becoming saints through to their bones. "Filled with all the fulness of God" (Ephesians 3:19) is an experience so great and so glorious that it makes the head of the modern saints so dizzy they are afraid to look up to those heavenly heights or peer down into the fathomless depths. Paul passes us on to Him, "that is able to do exceeding abundantly above all that we ask or think" (Ephesians 3:20). Paul knew how God answers prayer. This is a specimen of his teaching on prayer.

Two Types Of Teachers

In writing to the Philippian church, Paul recounts an event and shows the transmuting power of prayer as follows:

"Some indeed preach Christ of envy and strife; and some also of good will:

"The one preach Christ of contention, not sincerely, supposing to add affliction to my bonds:

"But the other of love, knowing that I am set for the defense of the gospel.

"What then? notwithstanding, every way, whether in pretense, or in truth, Christ is

102

preached; and I therein do rejoice, yea, and will rejoice.

"For I know that this shall turn to my salvation through your prayer, and the supply of the Spirit of Jesus Christ,

"According to my earnest expectation and my hope, that in nothing I shall be ashamed, but that with all boldness, as always, so now also Christ shall be magnified in my body, whether it be by life, or by death" (Philippians 1:15-20).

Boldness was to be secured by him in answer to their prayers. Christ was to be gloriously magnified by and through Paul, whether he lived or died.

Note that in all of these quotations in Corinthians, Ephesians, or Philippians, the Revised Standard Version gives us the most intense form of prayer, supplications. Paul requests intense, personal, strenuous, persistent praying by the saints. They must give special strength, interest, time, and heart to their praying to influence God to grant the most fruitful answers.

Pray Continually

The general instruction about prayer to the Colossian Christians is made specific and is sharpened to the point of a personal appeal: "Continue in prayer, and watch in the same, with thanksgiving; Withal praying also for us, that God would open unto us a door of utterance, to speak the mystery of Christ, for which I am also in bonds: That I may make it manifest, as I ought to

103

speak" (Colossians 4:2-4).

Paul is credited with the authorship of the epistle to the Hebrews. It gives the reader a reference to the character of Christ's praying, illustrating with authority the elements of true praying. How rich are his words! How heart-affecting and how sublime was His praying. He prayed as man never prayed before, and yet he prayed in order to teach man how to pray and how to receive from God. "Who in the days of His flesh, when He had offered up prayers and supplications with strong crying and tears unto Him that was able to save Him from death, and was heard in that He feared" (Hebrews 5:7).

The praying of Jesus Christ drew on the mightiest forces of His being. His prayers were His sacrifices, which He offered before He offered Himself on the cross for the sins of mankind. Prayer-sacrifice is the forerunner and pledge of self-sacrifice. We must die in our closets before we can die on the cross.

Chapter 13

EXAMPLES OF EFFECTIVE PRAYER

"One day Frank Crossley said good-bye to his friends, General and Mrs. Booth at the station. But before they steamed out, he handed a letter to them giving details of a sacrifice he had resolved to make for the (Salvation) Army. He came home and was praying alone. 'As I was praying,' he said, 'there came over me the most extraordinary sense of joy. It was not exactly in my head, nor in my heart, it was almost a grasping of my chest by some strange hand that filled me with an ecstasy I never had before. This was the joy of the Lord.' So this servant of God grew closer to Him. He thought it likely at the time that the Booths had read this letter in the train and his experience was God's answer to their prayer. He heard later that they had prayed for him in the train just after leaving Manchester"—Rev. Edward Shillito.

He who studies Paul's praying, both his prayers and his commands about prayer, will find it covers a wide, general, minute, and diversified area.

Famous spiritual leaders like Wesley, Brainerd, Luther, and others spent many hours in prayer. They committed all things—secular, religious, natural, and spiritual—to God in prayer. In this way they ordered their lives around God's provision and will. Yet, they were not superstitious or fanatics. In this they were only following the great example and authority of the apostle Paul.

To seek God as Paul did, by prayer, to commune with God as Paul did, to entreat Jesus Christ as Paul did, to seek the Holy Spirit by prayer as Paul did, to pray without ceasing—all this makes a saint, an apostle, and a leader for God. This kind of a life engages, absorbs, enriches, and empowers with God and for God. Prayer, if successful, will always engage and absorb us. This kind of praying brings the results and gifts that Paul experienced. Praying like Paul costs a lot. It is death to self, the flesh, and the world. Yet, the benefits of praying like Paul are worth the expense. Prayer which costs nothing gets nothing. It is a beggarly effort at best.

High Esteem For Prayer

Paul's respect of prayer is seen and enforced by the fact that Paul was a man of prayer. His high position in the Church was not one of the dignity and position in which he could enjoy himself and luxuriate. It was not one of officialism, nor was it one of arduous and exhaustless drudgery, for Paul was preeminently a praying man who got answers.

He began his great career for Christ in the great

struggle and school of prayer. God's convincing and wonderful argument to assure Ananias was, "Behold, he prayeth" (Acts 9:11). Three days he was without sight, neither eating nor drinking, but he learned the lesson well.

He went out on his first great missionary trip under the power of fasting and prayer. Paul and Barnabas established every church by the very same means—fasting and prayer. He began his work in Philippi "where prayer was wont to be made" (Acts 16:13). As "we went to prayer" (Acts 16:16), God answered by casting the spirit of divination out of the young woman. And when Paul and Silas were put in prison, they prayed and sang praises to God at midnight. In response, God took them out of prison.

Paul made praying a habit, a business, and a life. He literally gave himself to prayer. So with him praying was not a mere coloring, a paint, or a polish. Praying supplied the substance, the bone, and the marrow of his religious life. His conversion was a marvel of grace and power. His apostolic commission was full and royal. Paul knew that answered prayer was the key to making his ministry successful. Even though he had a dramatic conversion, Paul knew his apostolic mission was sealed by divine authority. Through prayer Paul accomplished his work, crowned his work, his life, and his death with martyr principles and with martyr glory.

Inclination To Pray

Paul's marked spiritual trait was a strong tendency to pray. He had a profound conviction that prayer was a great and solemn duty. Prayer was a royal privilege. Prayer gauged piety and made faith mighty. God expected Christians to pray, so He made prayer the key to Christian success through His answers.

Paul took it for granted that men who knew God would pray. He also knew that men who did not pray did not live for God. He revered prayer and knew its full value. Paul was in the habit of praying because he loved God, and such love in the heart always finds its expression in regular prayer. He felt his need for grace knowing that God only supplies grace through prayer. Grace only abounds more and more as prayer abounds more and more.

Paul, though in the habit of praying, did not pray by mere force of habit. Man is such a creature of habit that he is always in danger of doing things without thinking, in a routine, perfunctory manner. Paul's habit was regular and hearty. To the Romans he writes, "For God is my witness. . .that without ceasing I make mention of you always in my prayers" (Romans 1:9).

Prison doors are opened and earthquakes take place by praying such as Paul's. All things are opened to the kind of praying which was done by Paul and Silas. They could stop Paul from preaching, but they could not keep him from praying.

And the gospel could win its way by Paul's praying as well as by Paul's preaching. The apostle may have been in prison, but the Word of God was free and went like the mountain air, even though the apostle was bound in prison and abounded in prayer.

How profound their joy in Jesus which expressed itself so happily and so sweetly in praise and prayer, under conditions so painful and so depressing! Prayer brought them into full communion with God which made all things radiant with the divine presence. Prayer also enabled them to be "rejoicing that they were counted worthy to suffer shame for His name" (Acts 5:41) and to "count it all joy when they fell into divers temptations" (James 1:2). Prayer sweetens all things and sanctifies all things. A praying saint will be a praising saint. Praise is prayer set to music and song.

After that notable charge to the elders at Ephesus, as he visited there before continuing on his way to Jerusalem, this characteristic record is made:

"And when he had thus spoken, he kneeled down, and prayed with them all. And they all wept sore, and fell on Paul's neck, and kissed him" (Acts 20:36-37).

"He kneeled down and prayed." Note those words. Kneeling in prayer was Paul's favorite position, the fitting posture of an earnest, humble servant. Humility and intensity are appropriate for answered prayer from Almighty God. It is the proper attitude of man before God, of a sinner before a Savior, and of a beggar before his benefactor. To seal his sacred and living charge to those Ephesian elders by prayer was that which made the charge efficient, benign, and abiding.

The Missionary Call

Paul's religion was born in the throes of the three days' struggle of prayer while he was in the house of Ananias. There he received a divine impetus which never slackened till it brought him to the gates of the eternal city. That spiritual history and religious experience, coupled with unceasing prayer, brought him to the highest spiritual altitudes and yielded the largest spiritual results.

Paul lived in the very atmosphere of prayer. His first missionary trip was projected by prayer. It was in answer to prayer and fasting that he was called into the foreign missionary field. By the same means the church at Antioch was moved to send forth Paul and Barnabas on their first missionary journey. Here is the Scripture record of it:

"Now there were in the Church that was at Antioch certain prophets and teachers; as Barnabas, and Simeon that was called Niger, and Lucius of Cyrene, and Manean, which had been brought up with Herod the tetrarch, and Saul.

"As they ministered to the Lord, and fasted, the Holy Ghost said, Separate me Barnabas and Saul for the work whereunto I have called them.

"And when they had fasted and prayed, and laid their hands on them, they sent them away" (Acts

13:1-3).

Here is a model for all missionary outgoings, a forerunner of success. The Holy Spirit, in answer to prayer, directed an obedient church into divine leadership. This condition of things brought forth the very largest possible results in the mission of these two men of God. We may confidently assert that no church in which Paul was prominent was a prayerless church. Paul lived, toiled, and suffered in an atmosphere of prayer. To him, prayer was the very heart and life of religion, its meat and bone, the motor and the sign by which it conquered. Here is the divine record of Paul's work and the important role prayer played in establishing churches:

"Confirming the souls of the disciples, and exhorting them to continue in the faith, and that we must through much tribulation enter into the kingdom of God.

"And when they had ordained them elders in every church, and had prayed with fasting, they commended them to the Lord, on whom they believed" (Acts 14:22-23).

In obedience to a heavenly vision, Paul landed in Europe and found himself at Philippi. There was no synagogue, and few if any Jews lived there. A few pious women, however, had a meeting place for prayer, and Paul was drawn by spiritual guidance to the place "where prayer is wont to be made" (Acts 16:13). And Paul's first planting of the gospel in Europe was at that little prayer meeting. He was the chief person who prayed and the leading speaker. Lydia was the first convert at that prayer meeting. They extended the meeting, and they called it a meeting for prayer.

It was on the way to that extended prayer meeting that Paul performed the miracle of casting the devil of divination out of a poor demon-possessed girl. This poor girl had been made a source of gain by some covetous men. The results of Paul's deeds by the magistrate's orders was scourging and imprisonment. The result by God's orders was the conversion of the jailer and his whole household. The praying apostle allowed no discouragements.

Prayer Brings Salvation To Prison

In this last incident, we have a picture of Paul at midnight. He was in the inner prison, dark and deadly. He had just been severely whipped, his clothing was covered with blood, and there were blood clots on his torn body. His feet were in the stocks, and every nerve was feverish, swollen, and sensitive.

But, even under these very unfavorable and suffering conditions, he was absorbed in his favorite pursuit, confident of obtaining an answer. Paul was praying with Silas, his companion, in joyous, triumphant agreement. "And at midnight Paul and Silas prayed, and sang praises unto God: and the prisoners heard them. And suddenly there was a great earthquake, so that the foundations of the prison were shaken: and immediately all the doors were opened, and every one's bonds were loosed. And the keeper of the prison awaking out of his sleep, and seeing the prison doors open, he drew out his sword, and would have killed himself, supposing that the prisoners had been fled. But Paul cried out with a loud voice, saying, Do thyself no harm: for we are all here'' (Acts 16:25-28).

Never was prayer so beautiful, never more productive. Paul was adept at prayer. He was a lover of prayer who could pursue it with joy even under conditions of despondency and despair. What a mighty weapon of defense was prayer to Paul! How songful! The angels doubtless stilled their highest and sweetest notes to listen to the music which bore those prayers to heaven. The earthquake trod along the path made by the mighty forces of Paul's praying.

He did not escape when his chains were loosed and the stocks fell off. God answered Paul's prayers by showing him nobler purposes that night than his own individual freedom. His praying and the earthquake alarm were to bring salvation to that prison, freedom from the slavery of sin which was foreshadowed by his physical emancipation. God's mighty providence opened his prison door and broke his prison bonds, not only to give Paul freedom, but to give the jailer freedom as well. God's providential openings are often to test our ability to stay rather than to go. It tested Paul's ability to stay.

Chapter 14

BENEFITTING FROM PERSISTENT PRAYER

"William Law has said, 'When you begin your petitions use such various expressions of the attributes of God as may make you most aware of the greatness and power of His divine nature.' I want to emphasize and commend the principle of it, which is that our fellowship should begin with the primary elements of adoration and praise"—Rev. J.H. Jowett.

There are two occasions when, although Scripture does not explicitly say that Paul was in prayer, the circumstances and Paul's praying habit make it evident that the results obtained were God's answer to his prayer. The first occasion was when Paul sailed from Philippi and came to Troas where he stayed seven days. On the first day of the week, when the disciples came together to break bread, Paul preached to them late in the night, expecting to depart the next morning.

Sitting in the window was a young man named Eutychus, who fell asleep and fell out of the high window. Everyone believed he was dead. Paul went down to where the young man had fallen, and, embracing him, he told the people that they need not be troubled for life was still in the body. Paul returned to the upper room, where he had been preaching, and talked with the disciples till morning. The young man lived, and, as a consequence, all were greatly comforted.

The natural conclusion, without the fact being specifically stated, is that Paul must have prayed for the young man when he embraced him. His prayer was answered in the quick recovery of the young man.

Paul's Prayer Answers

The second occasion was in the long perilous storm which overtook the vessel in which Paul was being carried, as a prisoner, to Rome. They were tossed about in the great storm and neither sun nor stars appeared as they struggled against wind and storm. All hope of survival seemed gone.

But after a long absence, most likely in prayer, Paul stood in the midst of those on board and spoke particularly to the officers of the vessel, saying, "Sirs, ye should have hearkened unto me, and not have loosed from Crete, and to have gained this harm and loss. And now I exhort you to be of good cheer: for there shall be no loss of any man's life among you, but of the ship. For there stood by me this night the angel of God, whose I am, and whom I serve, Saying, Fear not, Paul; thou must be brought before Caesar: and, lo, God hath given thee all them that sail with thee. Wherefore, sirs, be of good cheer: for I believe God, that it shall be even as it was told me" (Acts 27:21-25).

It requires no strained interpretation to read into this simple record that Paul must have been praying when the angel appeared to him with that message of encouragement and assurance of safety. Paul's habit of prayer and his strong belief in prayer must have driven him to his knees. Such an emergency would necessarily move him to pray, especially since he was certain God would respond to him.

After the shipwreck, while on the island of Melita, Paul prayed again. He was praying for a very sick man. While a fire was being made, a deadly, poisonous snake fastened itself on his hand. The barbarians immediately concluded this was a case of retribution for some crime Paul had committed. But they soon discovered that Paul did not die. They then changed their minds concluding that he was a sort of god.

During his stay on the island, Publius' father was near death suffering from a hemorrhage and fever. Paul went to him, laid his hands upon him, and, with simple confidence in God, he prayed. Immediately, the disease was rebuked, and the man was healed. When the natives of the island saw this remarkable incident, they brought others to Paul, and they, too, were healed in answer to Paul's praying.

Earlier in Paul's life, when he was traveling from Ephesus on his way to Jerusalem, he stopped at Tyre. Before leaving Ephesus he had prayed with the Christians. But he did not trust in his words alone. God had to be recognized, invoked, and sought. Paul did not take it for granted, after he had done his best, that God simply would bless his efforts to do good. Paul sought God. God does not do things in a matter-of-course way. God must first be asked and consulted, then He will respond.

Following his visit to Ephesus, Paul arrived at Tyre, where he rested a few days. Here Paul found some disciples who begged him not to go to Jerusalem, saying through the Spirit that he should not go up to that city. But Paul adhered to his original purpose to go to Jerusalem. The account says:

"And when we had accomplished those days, we departed and went our way; and they all brought us on our way, with wives and children, till we were out of the city: and we kneeled down on the shore and prayed" (Acts 21:5).

What a sight to see on that seashore! Here is a picture of family love and devotion, where husbands, wives, and even children are present and praying out in the open air. What an impression it must have made upon those children! The boat was ready to depart, but prayer had to cement their affections, sanctify their wives and children, and bless their parting—a parting which was final so far as this world was concerned. The scene was beautiful and honored the head and heart of Paul. It showed the tender affection in which he was held. His devoted habit of sanctifying all things by prayer came directly to light. "We kneeled down on the shore, and prayed" (Acts 1:5). Never did anyone see a grander picture or witness a lovelier sight—Paul on his knees on the sands of that shore invoking God's blessing upon these men, women, and children.

When Paul was arraigned at Jerusalem, he referred to two instances of his praying in making his public defense. One instance was when he was in the house of Judas, in Damascus, after Jesus struck him to the earth and brought him under conviction. He was in Damascus three days when Ananias came to lay his hand upon him. This is the Scriptural record, and the words are those of Ananias addressed to Paul:

"And now why tarriest thou? arise, and be baptized, and wash away thy sins, calling on the name of the Lord" (Acts 22:16).

The Lord had emboldened the timid Ananias to go and minister to Paul, by telling him, "Behold, he prayeth" (Acts 9:11). And so we have in this reference Paul's prayerfulness intensified by the exhortation of Ananias. Prayer precedes pardon of sins. Prayer fits those who seek God. Prayer belongs to the earnest, sincere inquirer after God. Pardon of sin and acceptance with God always comes in answer to earnest praying. The evidence of sincerity in a true seeker of Jesus is that it can be said of him, "Behold, he prayeth."

The other reference in his defense lets us see the prayerful intensity with which his whole religious life had been fashioned. It shows how, in the absorbing ecstasy of prayer, the vision came and directions were given by which his toilsome life was to be guided. We also see the familiar terms on which he stood and talked with his Lord:

"And it came to pass, that, when I was come again to Jerusalem, even while I prayed in the temple, I was in a trance;

"And saw Him saying unto me, Make haste, and get thee quickly out of Jerusalem: for they will not receive thy testimony concerning Me.

"And I said, Lord, they know that I imprisoned and beat in every synagogue them that believed on Thee:

"And when the blood of Thy martyr Stephen was shed, I also was standing by, and consenting unto his death, and kept the raiment of them that slew him.

"And He said unto me, Depart: for I will send thee far hence unto the Gentiles" (Acts 22:17-21).

Prayer always brings directions from heaven as to what God would have us do. If we prayed more directly, we would make fewer mistakes in life as to duty. God's will concerning us is revealed in answer to prayer. If we prayed more, prayed better and sweeter, then we would receive clearer and more entrancing vision, and our walk with God would be of the most intimate, free, and bold order.

Paul's Prayers Were Comprehensive

It is difficult to itemize or classify Paul's praying. It is so comprehensive and detailed that it is no easy task to classify them. Paul taught a lot about prayer in his didactics. He specifically enforced the duty and necessity of prayer upon the Church. He practiced what he preached. He tested the exercise of prayer which he urged upon the people of his day.

To the church at Rome he plainly, specifically, and solemnly affirmed his habit of praying. He wrote this to those Roman believers:

"For God is my witness, whom I serve with my spirit in the gospel of His Son, that without ceasing I make mention of you always in my prayers" (Romans 1:9).

Paul not only prayed for himself. He made a practice of praying and seeking God's answers for others. He was first and foremost an intercessor. As he urged intercessory prayer on others, so he interceded for others.

He began that remarkable epistle to the Romans with prayer. He then closed it with this solemn charge: "Now I beseech you, brethren, for the Lord Jesus Christ's sake, and for the love of the Spirit, that ye strive with me in your prayers to God for me" (Romans 16:30).

But this was not all. In the very heart of that epistle, he commanded, "continuing instant in prayer" (Romans 12:12). That is, give constant attention to prayer. Make it the business of life. Be devoted to it. He recommended just what he did himself, for Paul was a standing example of the doctrine of prayer which he advocated and pressed upon the people.

In his epistles to the Thessalonians, how all-inclusive and wonderful the praying! He says in writing his first epistle to this church:

"We give thanks to God always for you all, making mention of you in our prayers; remembering without ceasing your work of faith, and labour of love, and patience of hope" (1 Thessalonians 1:2-3).

Not to quote all he says, it is worthwhile to read his words to this same church of true believers further on:

"Night and day praying exceedingly that we might see your face, and might perfect that which is lacking in your faith. Now God Himself. . .direct our way unto you. And the Lord make you to increase and abound in love one toward another. . .even as we do toward you: To the end He may establish your hearts unblameable in holiness before God, even our Father" (1 Thessalonians 3:10-13).

And this sort of praying for these Thessalonian Christians was in direct line with that closing prayer for those same believers in this epistle, where he recorded that striking prayer for their entire sanctification:

"And the very God of peace sanctify you wholly; and I pray God your whole spirit and soul and body be preserved blameless unto the coming of our Lord Jesus Christ" (1 Thessalonians 5:23).

How Paul prayed for those early Christians! They were in his mind and on his heart, and he was "night and day praying exceedingly." Oh, if only we had a legion of preachers, in these days of superficial piety and these times of prayerlessness, who would pray for their churches as Paul did for those early churches! Praying men are needed. Likewise praying preachers are demanded in this age.

At the conclusion of the remarkable prayer in the third chapter of Ephesians, he declared that God "is able to do exceeding abundantly above all that we ask or think" (Ephesians 3:20). In other words, God answers prayer abundantly. Paul earnestly desired to pray parallel to God's will taking full advantage of His power in order to bless and greatly enrich His Church.

Paul and his friends prayed for the saints everywhere. With what solemnity did Paul call the attention of the Roman Christians to the important fact of praying for them—believers whom he had never seen! "God is my witness. . .that without ceasing I make mention of you always in my prayers" (Romans 1:9). To the churches he said, "Praying always for you" (Colossians 1:3).

Again on the same theme we hear him articulating clearly, "Always in every prayer of mine for you all making request with joy" (Philippians 1:4). Again he wrote, "I do not cease to pray for you" (Colossians 1:9). Once more we read the record, "Wherefore also we pray always for you" (2 Thessalonians 1:11). And again it is written, "Cease not to give thanks for you, making mention of you in my prayers" (Ephesians 1:16). And then he said, "Remembrance of thee in my prayers night and day" (2 Timothy 1:3).

His declaration, "night and day praying exceedingly," is a condensed record of the engrossing nature of the praying done by this apostle. It shows conclusively how important praying and receiving answers was to him and to his ministry. It further shows how prayer was an agony of *earnest striving*, seeking blessings from God which could be secured no other way.

Chapter 15

CHURCH BODY PRAYERS
ARE NECESSARY

"I desire above all things to learn to pray. We want to sound the trumpet for the Christian warriors. We desire to find out why there is a lack of real praying. What is it? Why is it? Why so little time spent in prayer when Christ, who had command of His time, chose to spend great part of it in intercession? 'He ever liveth to make intercession for us' (Hebrews 7:25). We believe the answer is that the desire exists in the heart, but the will is undisciplined. The motive is present, but the affections have not melted under hours of heavenly meditation. The intellect is keen, yet not sharp enough for hours of tireless research. The intellect and the affections have never been linked together by the sealing of the blessed Holy Spirit for God's glory in the secret places, with doors shut, lusts crucified"—Rev. Homer W. Hodge.

Paul's many requests for prayer for himself, from those to whom he ministered, showed that

Paul had a high esteem for prayer because he knew the source of help. Paul prayed often himself and tried hard to teach Christians the extreme importance of the work of prayer. He felt the need of receiving answers to prayer so deeply that he believed firmly in the habit of personal praying. Realizing this for himself, he urged this invaluable duty upon others. Intercessory prayer, or prayer for others, was the most valuable type of prayer to Paul. It was no surprise, therefore, when he threw himself upon the prayers of the churches to whom he wrote.

Paul Depended On Believer's Prayers

Because of their devotion to Jesus Christ, their interest in the advancement of God's Kingdom on earth, and the ardor of their personal attachment to Jesus, he charged them to pray often. He wanted them to pray unceasingly in all things. Then realizing his own dependence on prayer to support his difficult duties, severe trials, and heavy responsibilities, he urged those to whom he wrote to pray especially for him.

The chief of the apostles needed answers to prayer. He needed the prayers of others, and he admitted this when asking for their prayers. His call to the apostleship did not lift him above this need. He realized and acknowledged his dependence on prayer. He craved and prized the prayers of all Christians. He was not ashamed to solicit prayers for himself nor to urge the brethren everywhere to pray for him.

In writing to the Hebrews, he based his request for prayer on two reasons: his honesty and his desire to visit them. If he were insincere, he could lay no claim to their prayers. Praying for him was a powerful agent in facilitating his visit to them. They touched the secret place of the wind and the waves, and, through prayer, God arranged all secondary agencies making them minister to this end.

Paul's frequent request of his brethren was that they would pray for him. One can judge the value of a thing by the frequency of its request and the urgent plea made for it. Since that was true with Paul, the prayers of the saints were among his greatest assets. By the urgency and reiteration of the request, "Pray for me," Paul showed conclusively the great value he put on prayer as a means of grace. Paul had no need more pressing than his need of prayer. He claimed prayer was the greatest factor behind the success of his work. Thus the most powerful and far-reaching energy in Paul's estimate was prayer. The intensity of his belief showed itself in these requests. In this entreaty for prayer he was writing to the Romans:

"I beseech you, brethren, for the Lord Jesus Christ's sake, and for the love of the Spirit, that ye strive together with me in your prayers for me" (Romans 15:30).

Prayers by others for Paul were valuable because they helped him. Nothing gives us so much aid in our need as real prayers. Through prayers, God supplies our needs and delivers us from difficulties. Paul's faith, so he wrote to the Corinthians, was often tested. He was comforted by his confidence that God would always deliver and strengthen him, especially in response to prayer. "Ye also helping by prayer" (2 Corinthians 1:11). God has done marvelous things for His favored saints through the prayers of others! The saints can help each other more by fervent praying than in any other way.

In the midst of envy, backbiting, and perils at the hands of false brethren, he wrote to the Philippians:

"For I know that this shall turn to my salvation through your prayer, and the supply of the Spirit of Jesus Christ,

"According to my earnest expectation and my hope, that in nothing I shall be ashamed, but that with all boldness, as always, so now also Christ shall be magnified in my body, whether it be by life, or by death" (Philippians 1:19-20).

Shame was taken away, holy boldness secured, and life and death made glorious in answer to the prayers of the saints at Philippi for Paul.

Prayer Brings Results

Paul had many mighty events occur during his ministry. His remarkable conversion was a great event, a powerful point of thrust. Yet, he did not secure results in his ministry because of the force of his astounding conversion. His call to the apostleship was clear, luminous, and all-convincing, but he knew he had to pray in order to bring the largest results in his ministry.

Paul's course was more clearly marked out and his career rendered more powerfully successful by prayer than by any other force.

Paul urged the Roman Christians to pray for him that he could be delivered from the negative effect of unbelieving men. Prayer is a defense and protection against the slander of evil men. Paul not only had unbelieving enemies with whom to contend, but there were many Christians who were prejudiced against him so much that it was doubtful whether they would accept any Christian service at his hands. This was especially the case at Jerusalem. Prayer, powerful prayer, had to be used to remove the mighty and pernicious force of inflamed and deep-seated prejudice. The Romans prayed that Paul would have a safe and prosperous journey so that God's answer would result in their mutual blessing and refreshment.

Paul's prayer requests were many-sided and all-comprehensive. How many things did his request to the Roman church include! The request for their prayers, like the church to whom it was directed, was cosmopolitan. He entreated them, a term indicating intensity and earnestness, "for the sake of Jesus Christ, to strive with him in their prayers for him." These prayers helped to deliver him from the evil men who could have hindered and embarrassed him in his mission. He wanted all of the brethren to accept his service to the poor saints, and he wanted to have the opportunity to visit the Roman church.

How full of earnestness was his request! How

tender and loving was his appeal! How touching and high was the motive for the highest and truest form of prayer, "for the Lord Jesus Christ's sake!" Also pray out of the love we bear for the Holy Spirit, the love which the Holy Spirit bears for us, and by the ties of the Christian brotherhood. He urged them to pray with these noble motives and to strive with him in their mutual praying. Paul was in the greatest prayer struggle, a struggle in which the mightiest issues were involved and imperiled. He was committed to the struggle because Christ was in it. He needed the help which comes only through answered prayer. So he pleaded with his brethren to pray for him and with him.

Prayer's Powerful Influence

Prayer will sweep enemies out of the way. Prayer will drive out the prejudices in the hearts of good men. His way to Jerusalem was cleared of difficulties, the success of his mission was secured, and the will of God and the good of the saints was accomplished. All these marvelous ends were secured in answer to marvelous praying. Wonderful and worldwide are the results to be gained by mighty praying. If all apostolic successors prayed as Paul did, if all Christians in all ages placed the same value on prayer as did the apostolic men, how marvelous and divine the history of God's Church would have been! How unparalleled its success would have been! The glory of its millenium would have brightened and blessed the world ages ago.

We see in Paul's request his belief in the far-reaching power of prayer. Not that prayer is a talismanic magical force, nor that it is a fetish, but because it moves God to do things that it suggests. Prayer has no magic, potent charm in itself, but it is all-powerful because it gets the Omnipotent God to grant its request. A forerunner basic to all prayer, as expressed or understood by Paul, is that "ye strive together with me in your prayers to God for me" (Romans 15:30). Paul needed reinforcements in this prayer struggle as well as divine help in his striving. He was in the midst of the struggle and bore the brunt, but he solicited the help of others. Their prayers were needed to help him offer intense prayers.

Prayer is not inaptly called "wrestling" because it is an intense struggle. Prayer has the greatest hindrances, and it has the most persistent foes. Mighty, evil forces surge around the closets of prayer. Powerful enemies who are strongly entrenched are near where praying is done. Paul's praying was no feeble, listless act. In this thing he "put away childish things" (1 Corinthians 13:11). The commonplace and the tame were retired. Paul had to pray mightily to receive an answer, or not at all. Hell had to feel the mightiness of his prayer stroke and stagger under it, or he would not strike at all. The strongest graces and the manliest efforts were required. Paul needed strength for his praying. Courage was at a premium. Timid touches and fainthearted desires accomplished nothing in the mind of Paul. Enemies had to be faced and routed. Fields were to be won. In order to receive answers to prayer, the Christian must pray with unflagging force, just as the apostle Paul prayed.

Chapter 16

PRINCIPLES FOR PRAYER

"We announce the law of prayer as follows: A Christian's prayer is a joint agreement of the will, the mind, the emotions, the conscience, the intellect, working in harmony at white heat. The body co-operates under certain hygienic conditions to make the prayer long enough and at a high voltage to insure tremendous supernatural and unearthly results"—Rev. Homer W. Hodge.

Paul made a request to the church at Ephesus, which is found in the latter part of chapter six of his epistle to those Christians:

"Praying always with all prayer and supplication in the Spirit, and watching thereunto with all perseverance and supplication for all saints;

"And for me that utterance may be given unto me, that I may open my mouth boldly, to make known the mystery of the gospel,

"For which I am an ambassador in bonds: that therein I may speak boldly as I ought to speak" (Ephesians 6:18-20).

He labored and prayed for this church night and

132

day. As he drew a vivid picture of the Christian soldier, with his foes harassing him, he gave the churches the duty of praying especially for him.

To these Ephesian Christians he gave a comprehensive statement of the necessity, nature, and special benefits of prayer. The most important was that God answered prayer. Prayer was to be urgent, covering all times and embracing all kinds of places. Supplication had to be intense, the Holy Spirit had to be invoked, vigilance and perseverance were necessary, and the whole family of saints had to be involved.

Paul Needed Prayer Support

The purpose behind his request for prayer centered on his need to be able to talk with power, fluency, direction, and courage. Paul did not depend upon his natural gifts, but on those which came to him in answer to prayer. He was afraid he would be a dull, dry speaker or a hesitating stammerer. He urged these believers to pray that he might not only speak clearly, but freely and fully.

He wanted them to pray for his boldness. No quality seems more important for a preacher than boldness. It is that positive quality which does not take consequences into too much account, but with freedom and fullness meets the crisis, faces a present danger, and performs a present duty without fear. Boldness was one of the marked characteristics of apostolic preachers and apostolic preaching. They were brave men; they were fearless preachers. The record of their trials is the applause of their faith.

There are many chains which enslave the preacher. His very tenderness makes him weak. His attachment to his people tends to bring him into bondage. His personal fellowship, his obligations to his people, and his love for them all tend to hamper his freedom and restrain his delivery in the pulpit. There is constant need to be continually praying for the preacher's ability to speak boldly as he ought to speak! A congregation must pray, seeking God's answers to their prayers for their preacher.

The prophets of old were charged not to be afraid of the faces of men. Unafraid of the frowns of men, they were to declare the truth of God without apology, timidity, hesitancy, or compromise. The warmth and freedom of conviction and sincerity, the fearlessness of a vigorous faith, and, above all, the power of the Holy Spirit were all wonderful helpers and elements of boldness. These things should be sought with all earnestness by modern ministers of the gospel!

Meekness and humility are high virtues of utmost importance in the preacher, but these qualities do not at all negate boldness. This boldness is not the freedom of furious speech. It is not scolding or rashness. It speaks the truth in love. Boldness is not rudeness. Roughness dishonors boldness. Boldness is as gentle as a mother with a babe, but as fearless as a lion standing before its foe. Fear, in the mild and innocent form of timidity, or in the offensive form of cowardice, has no place in the true ministry. Humble but holy boldness is of the very first importance.

What hidden, mysterious, mighty entity can add courage to apostolic preaching and give bolder utterances to apostolic lips? There is one answer, and that is knowing God has chosen to respond to prayer.

What can so affect and dominate evil that the very results of evil will be changed into good? We have the answer in Paul's words again:

"Who delivered us from so great a death, and doth deliver: in whom we trust that He will yet deliver us; Ye also helping together by prayer for us" (2 Corinthians 1:10). "What then? notwithstanding every way, whether in pretense, or in truth, Christ is preached; and I therein do rejoice, yea, and will rejoice" (Philippians 1:18).

Prayer, The Door Of Utterance

We can see how the promises of God become real and personal with prayer. "All things work together for good to them that love God" (Romans 8:28). Here is a jeweled promise. Paul loved God, but he did not usually rest on that promise alone to work out its blessed results. For example, he wrote to the Corinthians describing his escape from peril: "(God) delivered us from so great a death. . .we trust that He will yet deliver us; Ye also helping together by prayer" (2 Corinthians 1:10-11). In other words, helping me by prayer, you help God make the promise strong and rich in realization.

Paul's prayer requests embraced "supplication for all saints" (Ephesians 6:18) but especially for apostolic courage for himself. He needed this courage just as all preachers called of God need it! God responded to prayer and opened doors for the apostles' labors, but at the same time He opened apostolic lips to utter, with bravery and truth, the gospel message.

Here he spoke to the church at Colosses:

"Withal praying also for us, that God would open unto us a door of utterance, to speak the mystery of Christ, for which I am also in bonds:

"That I may make it manifest as I ought to speak" (Colossians 4:3-4).

It would be appropriate for such a request to be made by a modern preacher to his congregation! Present day preachers need those things which Paul desired for himself!

As in his request to the Ephesians, Paul wanted a "door of utterance" given him, so that he could preach with the liberty of the Spirit, be delivered from being hampered in thought or delivery. Furthermore, he desired the ability to give the gospel in the clearest terms, without confusion of thought, and with force. Every preacher today should and could speak with these attributes if the church prayed expecting God to answer. Happy that preacher who ministers to a people who pray like this for him! He would be still happier if he inwardly felt, as he faced his responsible task realizing how much he needed these things, that he encouraged his people to pray for him!

God answers prayer and changes crosses, trials, and oppositions into blessings, causing them to work for good. "This shall turn to my salvation through your prayer" (Philippians 1:19), says Paul. Today the same things in the life of the preacher are changed into gracious blessings in the end, "ye also helping together by prayer" (2 Corinthians 1:11). Saintly praying really helped apostolic preaching and rescued apostolic men from many dire circumstances. This kind of praying in these days will bring similar results in faithful preaching done by brave, fearless ministers. Prayer for the preacher produces results as prayer by the preacher produces results. Two things are always factors in the life and work of a good preacher. First, he prays constantly, fervently, and persistently for those to whom he preaches. Secondly, the congregation prays continually for their preacher. What a blessed set of circumstances when the preacher and congregation pray for each other.

Paul sent this pressing request to the church at Thessalonica:

"Finally, brethren, pray for us, that the word of the Lord may have free course, and be glorified, even as it is with you;

"And that we may be delivered from unreasonable and wicked men" (2 Thessalonians 3:1-2).

Prayer Illuminates The Word

Paul had a race-course in mind where the racer pushed himself to reach the goal. Hindrances were in the way of his success and had to be removed, so that the racer could finally succeed and obtain the reward. The Word of the Lord is this racer, as preached by Paul. This Word is personified and there are serious impediments which hamper the running of the Word. It must have a free course. Everything in the way, opposing its running, had to be taken out.

These impediments to the Word of the Lord running and being glorified are found in the preacher himself, in the church to whom he ministers, and the sinners around him. The Word runs and is glorified when it has unobstructed access to the minds and hearts of those to whom it is preached. When sinners are convicted of sin, when they seriously consider the claims of God's Word on them, and when they are induced to pray for themselves asking for pardoning mercy, the Word is glorified. The Word is glorified when saints are instructed in religious experience, corrected of doctrine errors and mistakes in practice, when they are led to seek higher things, and when they pray for deeper experiences in the divine life.

Note, it is not the preacher who is glorified because of the wonderful success brought through the Word. It is not when people praise the preacher unduly and make much out of him because of wonderful sermons, great eloquence, and remarkable gifts. The preacher must remain in the background in all this work of glorification, even though he is the foremost object of all this praying.

Prayer is to do all these things. This is why Paul urged, entreated, and insisted, "Pray for us" (Hebrews 13:18). It was not so much prayer for Paul personally in his Christian life and religious experience as it was for him officially. He needed God to answer the prayers for his work as a gospel minister. His tongue had to be unloosed in preaching, his mouth unstopped, and his mind set free. Answers to prayer were not to help "work out his own salvation," but to help him live correctly and to effectively advertise the Word of the Lord. They would also keep him from hindering the Word as he preached, as he desired that no hindrance should be in himself which would defeat his own preaching.

He also wanted all hindrances taken away from the churches to whom he ministered so that church people would not stand in the way or weigh down the Word as it ran the race course attempting to reach the minds and hearts of people. Furthermore, he prayed that hindrances in the unsaved would be set aside so that, when he preached God's Word, it would reach their hearts and be glorified in their salvation.

Thinking all of these things, Paul sent his pressing request to the believers at Thessalonica, "Pray for us," because praying by true Christians would greatly help to spread the Word of the Lord.

The preacher who sees these things, realizing that his success depends largely on this kind of praying from his people, is wise. We need churches now which, having the preacher in mind and the Word on their hearts, pray for him that "the Word of the Lord may have free course, and be glorified" (2 Thessalonians 3:1).

One other item in this request is worth noting: "That we may be delivered from unreasonable and wicked men" (2 Thessalonians 3:2). Such men are hindrances in the way of the Word of the Lord. Many preachers are harassed by them and need to be delivered from them. Prayer helps to bring such a deliverance. Paul was annoyed by such characters, and for this reason he urged prayer for himself that he might find deliverance from them.

Evangelical Success Bound To Prayer

Summing it all up, we find that Paul felt the success of the Word, its liberty and largeness, were bound up in prayers, and he found that failure to pray would restrict the Word's influence and glory. His deliverance from unreasonable and wicked men as well as his safety depended upon their prayers and God's answers. These prayers, while they greatly helped him preach, at the same time protected him from the cruel plans of wicked and unreasonable men.